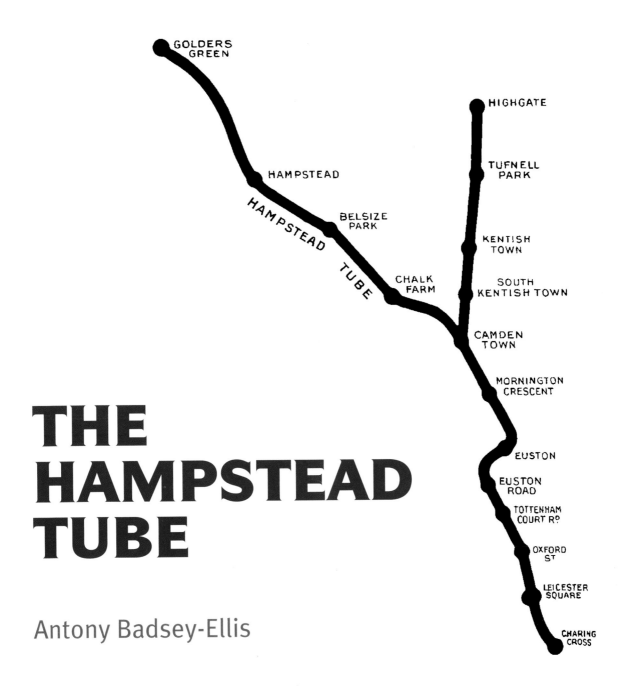

THE HAMPSTEAD TUBE

Antony Badsey-Ellis

Capital Transport

First published 2007

ISBN 978-1-85414-312-9

Published by Capital Transport Publishing
PO Box 250, Harrow, Middlesex, HA3 5ZH

Printed by Craft Print, Singapore

Photographic credits

London Transport Museum	4, 7, 18, 24, 27, 28, 29, 30 lower, 31, 32, 33 upper, 37, 40, 41, 42, 44, 45, 48, 52, 55, 56, 59, 60, 61, 62, 63, 64, 65, 67, 68, 69, 70 left, 71, 72, 73, 74, 77, 78, 86, 88, 91, 92, 93, 96, 102, 103, 109, 110, 112, 114, 117, 119, 123, 124, 125, 126, 132, 134, 137, 138
Aerofilms Ltd	66, 70 right
The Times	111
Memories	118
R. J. Greenaway	130
Capital Transport	131, 136, 142
London Underground Ltd	140, 141, 146
Brian Hardy	148

Pictures not credited are from the author's or publisher's collections.

The author and publisher would like to thank the staff of the National Archives, the London Metropolitan Archives, the Transport for London Archives, London Transport Museum Reference Library, and the Guildhall Library for their assistance with research. Brian Hardy and Mike Horne read through the manuscript and suggested a number of improvements to the accuracy of the text. Wendy Badsey-Ellis proof-read the draft and made useful comments that have improved the style and content.

CONTENTS

From the cover of the souvenir opening booklet for the Hampstead Tube.

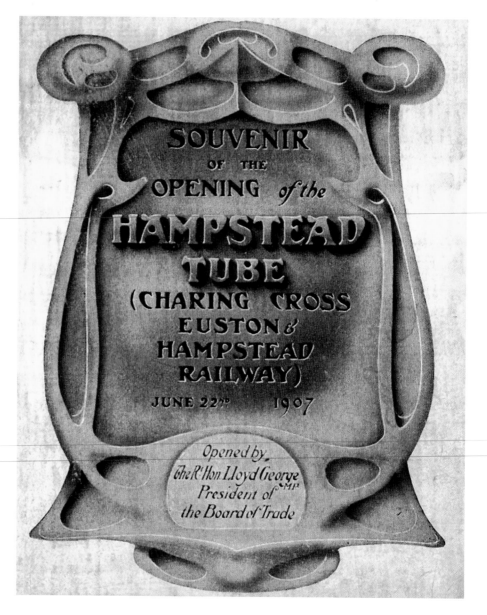

SOUVENIR
OF THE
OPENING of the
HAMPSTEAD
TUBE
(CHARING CROSS
EUSTON &
HAMPSTEAD
RAILWAY)
JUNE 22ᵗᴴ 1907

Opened by
the Rᵗ Hon Lloyd George MP
President of
the Board of Trade

INTRODUCTION

It is amazing to think that the Hampstead Tube was described as 'the last link', as if the Underground railways of London were complete when it opened 100 years ago. It was only two years after opening that its first extension was proposed, and since then it has become one-half of London's most complex tube line, the Northern.

The Hampstead was unique amongst the early tube railways in that it ventured to the surface in a rural district near London, two miles beyond its originally planned terminus of Hampstead, entirely as a result of a change in ownership and the new owner's belief (based on experience in the USA) that the houses would follow the railway. This was several years before the Metropolitan Railway proved the concept in London with the growth of what it called Metro-Land.

Saturday 22nd June 1907 was a cool, overcast day, with light winds driven from the south-west by high pressure over the Bay of Biscay. It was to see the opening of the Charing Cross, Euston & Hampstead Railway (CCE&HR), which was described by its promoters as the completion of the tube railways owned by the Underground Electric Railways of London (UERL). The last construction work had not yet been completed, and an unusual agreement was reached with the contractors. They would pay the operating costs and receive all receipts until 30th June.

To celebrate the occasion, free travel was provided for the public on the day of opening (what the *Railway Magazine* termed 'open tunnel'). The company provided 127,500 free tickets, but these ran out before the end of the day. Many thousands more passengers continued to be carried free of charge, and it was estimated that around 150,000 members of the public travelled between the opening at 13.30 and the close of traffic at 20.45. Passengers were requested not to bring young children along. To ensure that the day went smoothly, especially with the anticipated heavy traffic in the afternoon, the entire staff of the railway was on duty, as well as additional staff from other lines who were drafted in to help. Police were also on duty at every station to help with any overcrowding that occurred.

The ceremonies started with the President of the Board of Trade, David Lloyd George, starting a train at Charing Cross station using an engraved gold key which *The Mole*, a public newsletter that accompanied the line's opening, described as 'a massive gold spanner'. A similar ceremony held the previous year for the Piccadilly Tube had encountered problems when the gold key refused to fit, and Lloyd George had instead resorted to a standard train key. He might have felt that these occasions were jinxed, as a short delay occurred when he released the deadman's handle, bringing the train to a stop in the tunnel. The train was soon on the move again, and Lloyd

George and the company's directors and around 400 other guests were treated to a tour of the entire line, running first to Highgate station. The train reversed here, returning to Mornington Crescent, where it reversed again to travel the Hampstead branch up to Golder's Green. It is likely that Lloyd George operated the train until the first station at Leicester Square; a regular driver would then have taken over.

On arrival at Golder's Green the invited guests on board the train listened to a number of speeches, before settling down to enjoy a fine luncheon in the paint shop at the depot, which had been suitably decorated for the occasion.

The speeches commenced with the CCE&HR Chairman, Sir George Gibb, noting

> that it was in some ways the most important of the railways constructed by the Underground Electric Railways Company of London, in that it opened up Hampstead and Highgate, to which access had hitherto been somewhat inconvenient, and thus provided the people of London with new possibilities of living in the country.

Sir Edgar Speyer, who was Chairman of the UERL, followed this by describing some of the difficulties encountered in building the network of tube railways. He was surprised that there was still no central authority to manage traffic in London, and concluded by noting that London could well benefit from public ownership of the underground railways, of which he was in favour.

The guest of honour, Lloyd George, made the final speech in which he offered his congratulations to all involved in the tube railways, and indicated that the Government was indeed considering setting up some form of Traffic Board.

Luncheon was followed by the usual toasts, as well as 'Prosperity to the Charing Cross, Euston & Hampstead Railway' (by Lloyd George), and 'The Engineers, Architect, and Contractors' (by Speyer). A politician who was later to become chairman of the London Electric Railways company (described later), Lord George Hamilton, concluded with a toast to 'Our Guests'.

The publicity for the opening made no reference to extensions that had been authorized to Edgware and Watford; since the death of the American financier who had arranged the capital for the line in December 1905, a more cautious approach of consolidation was being taken by the UERL. Instead it heralded 'the last link of the new chain of communication'. The new symbol (what would today be called a logo) for the UERL featured prominently in the brochure, with its motto 'Swift and Sure'. Right from the start the company adopted the popular title of the Hampstead Tube, in a similar vein to the Bakerloo Tube title bestowed upon the Baker Street & Waterloo Railway by *The Evening News*. Some parts of the press attempted to call it the Charing Cross Tube, but this name did not stick.

The popularity of the day was demonstrated by the queues of people stretched down the Charing Cross cab road waiting for their free ride in the early afternoon. Six-car trains plied back and forth at 4-minute intervals. The *Railway Magazine* noted that 'if the travellers of Saturday, June 22nd, make and pay for a journey at least once every week, the Charing Cross, Euston and Hampstead Railway will have no occasion to regret their hospitality'.

Once they had experienced the new railway, some people headed for the Bull & Bush public house on the northern edge of Hampstead Heath to enjoy music from a band from 17.00 until 20.00, followed by an illuminated open-air concert at 20.15, and beautiful gardens illuminated with fairy lamps.

Opening of the
HAMPSTEAD TUBE
SATURDAY, JUNE 22, 1907.

ALIGHT AT
Golders Green

Five minutes' walk to

"Ye Olde Bull & Bush"

FOR

GOOD

Dinners and Teas

A BAND will play from 5 till 8.

OPEN-AIR CONCERT

In the Beautiful Gardens,
Illuminated with Fairy Lamps, at **8.15**

Admission 6d.   Numbered & Reserved Seat 1/-

Telephone: 1685 (P.O.) Hampstead.

The handbill distributed by the *Bull & Bush* public house to invite those attending the Hampstead Tube opening to their evening celebrations.

CHARING CROSS,
EUSTON & HAMPSTEAD
RAILWAY

Scale, 4 Inches to 1 Mile.

Authorised Stations shewn thus ●

London: G. W. Bacon & Co., Ltd., 127, Strand.

PLANNING THE RAILWAY

The story of the CCE&HR began over 15 years earlier, in 1891. The world's first tube railway, opened in December 1890, was the City & South London Railway (C&SLR). With six stations on a route linking King William Street (in the City of London) and Stockwell (to the south), it had proved to be an immediate sensation, and crowds flocked to use it. The cold winter of 1890 undoubtedly helped, with the prospect of waiting on an enclosed platform more enticing than standing in the frosty streets waiting for a horse-drawn omnibus. But there was also the love of innovation. The Victorian period was one of great change as Britain was crossed by an expanding network of railways. The public was used to the press telling them of the latest technological marvel. Now they could try something the likes of which they had never seen before – a railway running in tunnels deep beneath London without the noise, smoke and steam that locomotives usually produced. The trains were powered by another wonder of the age: electricity.

The success of the C&SLR caused a flurry of tube railway promotion. It had opened too late for Bills to be submitted for the 1891 parliamentary session, and so the engineers and promoters for these other lines had most of that year to work on their plans. Plans for four new tube railways were deposited with Parliament late in 1892: in response, it was decided that a joint select committee (i.e., one composed of members of both Houses of Parliament) would examine all of the schemes, allowing a consistent approach to be taken to them.

The new railways were:

Name	Length	From	To	Via
Baker Street & Waterloo	3 m 1.5 ch (4.86 km)	Baker Street	Waterloo	Oxford Circus and Charing Cross
Great Northern & City	3 m 3 f 8.1 ch (5.59 km)	Finsbury Park	Moorgate	Highbury
Hampstead, St Pancras & Charing Cross	5 m 5.65 ch (8.16 km)	Hampstead	Charing Cross (Strand)	Camden and Tottenham Court Road
Waterloo & City	1 m 4 f 6.8 ch (2.55 km)	Waterloo	Mansion House	(No intermediate stations)

Facing page The map published by the CCE&HR Company shortly after the line received Parliamentary approval in 1893.

9

The Hampstead, St Pancras & Charing Cross Railway changed its name to the Charing Cross, Euston & Hampstead Railway just prior to Royal Assent, which was given on 24th August 1893. Its promoters must have breathed a sigh of relief, as they had spent much of the previous two years working on the scheme, and had originally hoped to have approval the previous summer. Assent was given to the other three railways as well, but only the Waterloo & City had any success in raising the capital necessary to pay for the construction and equipment of their line, as it was backed by the main-line London & South Western Railway company.

The CCE&HR Act gave powers for the construction of a railway from Heath Street, in Hampstead, to Charing Cross, with a short branch diverging eastwards at the Euston Road. The branch would serve Euston and St Pancras stations, and allow trains to run to the southern terminus.

Due to the steep gradients (up to 1 in 24) at the Hampstead end of the line cable haulage was the method of propulsion originally intended. A continuous cable would move through the tunnels at a speed of 16 mph. The carriages would use gripper devices to fix themselves to the cable when they needed to move, and on the approach to stations the grippers would be released and the carriages would coast to a halt in the stations. A number of tramways around the world had used cable-haulage, and in London the C&SLR had originally planned to operate in the same way, until their cable contractors had gone into liquidation.

One of the changes made to the plan as it was considered by Parliament was to the St Pancras branch. The Midland Railway, owners of the main-line station at St Pancras, objected to the tunnels passing beneath their ornate Gothic building, and as a result the branch was cut back to Chalton Street, with Euston its only station.

The depot and power station for the line were permitted to be at either Chalk Farm or Hampstead. The former location had the advantage of easy access to coal from the main-line railway yard nearby; the latter was probably preferable for pulling the cars up the long steep gradient into the station.

Following Royal Assent a prospectus was issued to announce the scheme to the public, and hopefully to persuade them to purchase shares. Advertisements were placed in the *Financial Times* on 29th and 30th March 1894 describing the railway. Although any form of motive power other than steam was permitted, the promoters explained that they had now consulted their engineers and decided upon electrical traction. The advertisement went on to explain how, even with just 75 passengers per train each paying 1½d on average, the line would give an annual return of £86,620, or just over 6 per cent on the share capital. Eight directors were named, including Joseph Lyons, Joseph Browne Martin, and Edwin Levy (who were all Directors of the J. Lyons tea-room company). The company sought to issue £1,416,000 in shares of £10. Disappointingly for the promoters this was not a success, and at the Board meeting of 10th April 1894 they agreed to return the money to the subscribers as it was not sufficient for them to justify allotting the shares.

The lack of ability to raise money remained a theme of the 1890s, and not just for the CCE&HR; many new tube railways were proposed throughout the decade, and of the few that successfully obtained an Act of Parliament, almost all failed to raise the all-important capital. As the powers to construct and open the railway were limited in duration, the company directors were left having to promote occasional Bills to extend the available time. The CCE&HR successfully obtained Royal Assent for such measures in 1897, 1898, and 1900.

The Bill for 1898 also sought to change the southern end of the line. As originally authorized it curved east from the Charing Cross Road into what is now William IV Street, and along the Strand to Southampton Street. The changes for 1898 moved the terminus to Craven Street, on the western side of the main-line station at Charing Cross. Royal Assent was given on 24th July.

The next change was made in 1899. It was recognized that the short branch to Euston would make the operation of the line difficult, and that a major main-line station should not be placed off the principal route. The authorized line for the railway between Euston Road and Camden following the Hampstead Road was therefore abandoned, and the Euston branch was extended in a northwards curve up Eversholt Street. It rejoined the original route near the site of Mornington Crescent station (although this was not yet included in the railway).

Just as the original branch was removed from the plans a new one was added, diverging at Camden Town (where a new station was added), and leading to another new station at Kentish Town. A single intermediate station would be built at Castle Road, and a depot would be built on the surface north of the terminus. At the southern end of the line, Charing Cross station (under Craven Street) would be made 9ft closer to the surface.

Another station was added in 1899 at Cranbourn Street, between the southern terminus and the station at Oxford Street. It was to have interchange with the Brompton & Piccadilly Circus Railway (B&PCR), a tube scheme that was promoting a line from South Kensington to Piccadilly Circus. In 1899 the B&PCR put forward plans for an extension eastwards under Leicester Square to Cranbourn Street, where it would meet the CCE&HR. Interchange would be convenient, and so platforms were added to the latter railway scheme.

At the instigation of the London County Council (LCC) a clause was added to the 1899 Bill compelling the company to issue workmen's tickets, valid for travel in 3rd class, for a maximum fare of 1d single and 2d return (more detail of fares is given in a later chapter). These were to be valid on trains operated before 08.00, which were to call at all stations on the line. This was a standard request of the LCC, which campaigned tirelessly for better facilities for workmen on the railways. With the exception of the Great Northern & City Railway all of the tube railways constructed in London operated with a single class of carriage, in which the workmen's tickets were valid.

No substantial changes were made by Parliament, and the CCE&HR Act of 1899 was given Royal Assent on 9th August, as was the B&PCR Act.

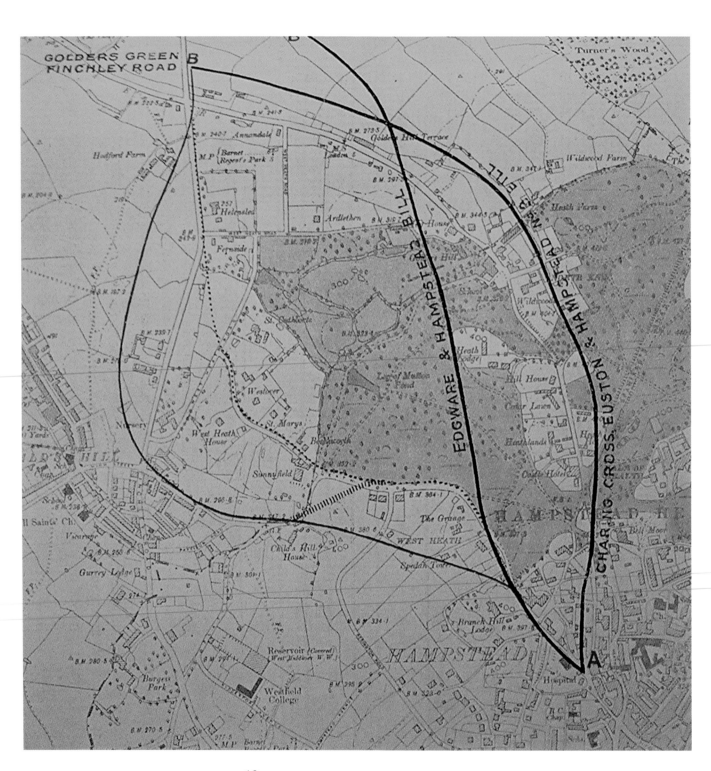

YERKES TAKES OVER

On 3rd December 1897 it was noted in the Minutes for the CCE&HR Board meeting that Robert Perks was in attendance. This was the first time that his name appears in the minutes, and was significant for the company. Perks was a solicitor with connections to the Metropolitan and Metropolitan District Railways, and was also MP for Louth. Over the next three years he planned the takeover of the CCE&HR in order that capital might be raised. Thus far this had been a singular failure, with just 451 shares being issued to eight people, and just £2 paid up on each. The total authorized capital of £1,776,000 was a long way off being realized.

The Times of 20th September 1900 noted that two men from New York, Arthur Houseman and Henry Davis, were in London, representing an American financier who was interested in the CCE&HR. Eight days later the Board Minutes recorded the following memorandum:

> Mr Perks explained the circumstances under which Mr Yerkes was paying over to the persons entitled £60,000 and taking a transfer of the Parliamentary deposit of £60,638.15.9, and it was resolved that the Company pay out of the funds of the Company when the Capital is raised a sum equal to 5% per annum upon the £60,000 advanced by Mr Yerkes after crediting the amount received by Mr Yerkes in respect of interest payable upon such deposit.

Charles Tyson Yerkes was an American financier who had built up the elevated railroad and tramway system in Chicago. His methods had sometimes been dubious, and it was not unknown for him to resort to bribery in order to achieve success. However, things became tougher for him; legislation that he had hoped would pass, granting him long-term franchises on the railways, was rejected by the Chicago City Council. Feeling the pressure, Yerkes sold up and moved his gaze to London.

Shortly before his departure from Chicago two of the promoters of the CCE&HR had been in America looking to raise the necessary funds to build the line, having given up hope of doing so in Britain. They met Yerkes, and offered to sell the powers for the railway to him for just $200,000 (£100,000) on one condition: that the construction would be carried out by a company owned by one of the promoters.

Yerkes sent Davis to London initially to determine the attractiveness of the railway scheme. When he reported back enthusiastically, the financier's right-hand man DeLancey Louderback was sent across the Atlantic as well, together with an engineer. Louderback was very impressed with the financial prospects for the line, and secured an option on the undertaking for Yerkes.

Facing page The map published by Hampstead residents in 1900 showing the routes of the two authorised railways, and their own preferred route to the west of Child's Hill (see p15 for more details).

It was now time for Yerkes to see the route for himself, and he arrived in London on 26th July 1900. He travelled the length of the route with Davis, before meeting Perks in the latter's office. Negotiations continued with the promoters, and before long the requirement to use the specified construction company was dropped: Yerkes had particularly objected to this, having made significant sums in the past from construction contracts.

The CCE&HR was his first purchase, with an agreement being signed between him and the railway company on 27th September 1900. The following day a meeting was held at the Charing Cross Hotel at which the railway was formally transferred to Yerkes, who took on the role of Chairman. Davis was elected as the Vice-Chairman. For a total outlay of £100,000 the powers for the railway belonged to Yerkes. The five existing directors had retired earlier to be replaced by men of Yerkes's choosing. Rather optimistically in September 1900 the Company reported to *The Times* that it felt the railway could be constructed and opened within two years.

Yerkes had realized that in order to maximize the traffic on the railway it would have to help generate it. To this end he looked beyond the northern terminus. The steep gradients towards Hampstead had not impressed his engineers, and by extending the line northwards to the hamlet of Golder's Green they could be considerably eased (although at the expense of making Hampstead station deeper). A depot and power station for the railway could be easily and cheaply constructed at this location as well. Yerkes also saw the potential of developing the land around the new terminus, which in 1900 was almost completely rural. One possibly apocryphal tale describes Yerkes and the engineer Harley Hugh Dalrymple-Hay taking a hansom cab along the route of the railway to Hampstead in autumn 1900. Yerkes decided to continue north to Golder's Green, and took the decision to extend the line on the spot. Dalrymple-Hay was less impressed, seeing little or no traffic potential in the lonely crossroads north of Hampstead Heath. Yerkes was made of stronger stuff though, having seen housing in the countryside around Chicago spring up along the routes of electric trolleycars that his companies had built in the 1890s.

A Bill was prepared for the 1901 parliamentary session seeking authorization for the extension, which was 1 mile 3 furlongs 3 chains (2.27 km) long. An area of land to the north-east of the crossroads was to be taken for the depot and power station for the line. There was considered to be potential for an intermediate station at Jack Straw's Castle.

Another Bill was also submitted for the same session. This contained two further extensions: the first taking the Kentish Town branch northwards to beneath Highgate main-line station (via the Archway Tavern), and the second extending the line south from Charing Cross to Victoria, via Whitehall and Parliament Square. Together these totalled 3 miles 5 furlongs 3.5 chains (5.90 km).

Twelve new tube railway Bills were deposited with Parliament at the end of 1900, a record number probably spurred on by the success of the Central London Railway (CLR), which had opened from Shepherd's Bush to Bank in July of that year. In order to manage this unprecedented demand, another joint select committee was created to consider them all in a fair and equitable manner, and make recommendations. The only comment made about the CCE&HR Bills was that the Kentish Town and Highgate branch should be operated as a shuttle service to avoid having a deep-level junction used by trains in passenger service. One of the recommendations from the joint select committee of 1901 had been that junctions on tube railways should be avoided. This was originally put forward by the Board of Trade (BoT), who wanted to avoid the risk of passenger trains in small tunnels deep below the ground coming into collision. The BoT made the same comments to the Windsor Committee of 1902.

Unfortunately for all of the railways involved, the Committee spent so long in its deliberations that there was insufficient time remaining to allow any of the Bills to go forward that year. Instead, special dispensation was granted allowing them to be carried over to the 1902 session. Of course, more Bills for new railways were also deposited for this session, bringing the total number of Bills for parliamentary consideration to 27 (as the 1901 Bills would have to be reconsidered to some degree). This time the House of Lords created two separate Committees; one to peruse the railways running east/west, chaired by Lord Windsor, and the other looking into those running north/south, chaired by Lord Ribblesdale. The CCE&HR fell into the latter group.

A third Bill had been deposited by the CCE&HR for 1902. This amended the route slightly in Hampstead, and moved the Charing Cross terminus from Craven Street (on the western side of the main-line station) to Villiers Street (on the eastern side). It was noted in the Board meeting of 24th January 1902 that this would afford better interchange with the Metropolitan District Railway (MDR). Another station was also added to the line, between Oxford Street and Euston Road (this new station is now called Goodge Street).

The Ribblesdale Committee deliberated the three Bills from the CCE&HR, and made a number of amendments. They noted that the extension to Victoria and the part of the northern extension between Archway Tavern and Highgate did not comply with Parliamentary Standing Orders, and thus rejected them. This left the two short northern extensions to Golder's Green and Archway Tavern, as well as the deviation at Charing Cross from their 1902 Bill to be considered.

The most contentious section was that beneath Hampstead Heath. The residents of Hampstead objected loudly to the intrusion of the tube, with vociferous opposition appearing in the pages of *The Times*. On 25th June 1900 the line was described by a correspondent as 'burrowing mole-like under the heath and throwing up stations to mark its track'. Exactly six months later an article, based on the petition of the Hampstead Heath Preservation Society (HHPS), made a series of bizarre claims about the effect of the new railway tunnel. Even though the tunnels were as deep as 221 feet below the surface, the HHPS feared that the trees would be shaken down by the vibration of the trains, and the water would be drained away from the vegetation. This view was ridiculed by the barrister representing the CCE&HR, who further observed that the railway would bring people to the Heath to enjoy it. The protesters continued to insist that the railway should be routed round the west side of the Heath, through Child's Hill, and on 23rd January 1901 a letter from Douglas Fox, the engineer for the railway, was published in response. He noted that only 320 yards of the line was beneath the Heath, that it was always at least 150ft deep, and that currently the company had powers to erect an electrical generating station in the centre of Hampstead. The implication was that surely the objectors would prefer this to be in Golder's Green, and therefore the tunnels were a small price to pay.

Part of the problem was that the CCE&HR was not alone in proposing a line between Hampstead and Golder's Green. A company by the name of the Edgware & Hampstead Railway (E&HR) had put forward a Bill for a line connecting the two points in its name, joining with the CCE&HR at Hampstead (the original northern terminus). It did not make sense to have duplicate railways, and the intention of the E&HR had always been that they would be a northward extension of the CCE&HR. An agreement was therefore reached between the two companies that they would connect at Golder's Green and the section of the E&HR to the south would be abandoned. The connection would have to wait for another Act of Parliament though.

On 16th July 1902 the Lords approved all four Bills, with the three CCE&HR Bills being merged into one. Royal Assent was received on 18th November the same year.

We now need to return to 1901, and the activities of Yerkes. Not satisfied with just the CCE&HR he went on to purchase substantial holdings in the Metropolitan District Railway. This was again at the instigation of Perks, himself an owner of a large number of MDR shares. The District, as it was frequently known, had never been in a good shape financially, and competition with the new tube railways showed that they would have to electrify their lines in order to remain competitive. The lack of capital prevented anything more than a small experiment, consisting of a single electric train operating between Earl's Court and High Street Kensington, and Perks realized that a new source of funding would have to be found.

By June 1901 Yerkes had spent over £1 million, but acquired shares with a face value far in excess of this, and in doing so secured control of the company. A separate undertaking, the Metropolitan District Electric Traction Company (MDETC) was formed with capital of £1 million. Its object was to electrify the District Railway and construct the necessary electrical generating station. This power house had been planned by a separate tube railway, the Brompton & Piccadilly Circus, on a site that could be expanded to provide power to several railways. As the B&PCR enjoyed a close relationship with the District it was not surprising when it soon came under the control of Yerkes as well.

Two more tube railways that had been authorized but were unable to raise funds were taken over by Yerkes in the course of the next nine months. In September 1901 the Great Northern & Strand Railway (GN&SR) was purchased, and promptly linked with the B&PCR to form a tube railway stretching across London from South Kensington to Finsbury Park. The name was also changed to the Great Northern, Piccadilly & Brompton Railway (GNP&BR). Finally, in March 1902 the half-built Baker Street & Waterloo Railway (BS&WR) was purchased for £360,000.

The MDETC was now seriously stretched for funds, and Yerkes turned to the London-based finance house of Speyer Bros to raise more capital. A new company was formed on 9th April 1902 with £5 million of capital, called the Underground Electric Railways Company of London Ltd (UERL). This absorbed the MDETC and its controlling interest in the five railway companies, including the CCE&HR. The UERL would be the contractor to construct all of its tube railways, allowing an unprecedented degree of standardization. The plan was now to supply electricity to all of the railways from a single generating station, to be located at Lots Road in Chelsea, on the north bank of the Thames. However, the individual railways retained a degree of autonomy, as demonstrated by the decision-making in mid-1904 about the source of electricity.

The CCE&HR was offered a contract for the supply of power from Lots Road. They commissioned their own engineer (H. F. Parshall) to investigate whether this would be complete in time, and whether it would be cheaper for them to erect their own power station at Elephant & Castle. However, Parshall concluded that this would not be economical, and so Lots Road was to be the source of power for the line.

Almost a year later Dalrymple-Hay was appointed to supervise the construction of the platforms at Charing Cross, a cable tunnel at Villiers Street, and the connected shafts. The tunnel and shafts were for the high-voltage cables from Lots Road which were routed via the MDR tunnels, as well as the cables bringing traction current from Charing Cross substation to the Hampstead Tube. The cable subway used part of the alignment for the railway beneath Villiers Street authorized in 1902, and led perpendicularly from the southern end of the northbound platform, past the end of the southbound platform, and then curved sharply under the roadway.

The Edgware & Hampstead Railway became part of the Yerkes empire on 25th March 1903, when a controlling interest was taken by the CCE&HR. Powers were now held for a continuous line from Charing Cross to Edgware, as well as the branch to Archway Tavern. The new northern terminus at Edgware was not seen as being the end of the line by some, and a Watford & Edgware Railway (W&ER) was successfully promoted by independent parties in 1903, despite opposition from the CCE&HR. Its promoters always intended it to operate as an extension of the E&HR, and so nothing was done by way of construction in the short term.

A view of the Lots Road power station under construction in 1903, reproduced from a contemporary magazine.

17

18

CONSTRUCTION

We now go back a few months to July 1902, when the construction works for the line began. The first signs of progress were the demolition of houses on Haverstock Hill, and more sites were cleared over the following months. The station sites at Leicester Square, Euston (on the corner of Melton and Drummond Streets), Camden Town, Chalk Farm, and Belsize Park were all ready for shafts to be sunk by April 1903. Five months later, the tunnelling began.

All of the running tunnels had an internal diameter of 11ft 8¼ins, except on the sharper curves where this was increased to 12ft 7ins to allow for the overhang at the ends of the cars as they passed around the curves. The station platform tunnels were 21ft 2½ins internal diameter. The tunnels were lined with cast-iron segments bolted together at the flanges. Compressed air was then used to force lime grout between the segments and the clay behind, preventing subsidence above and helping to secure the position of the tunnels.

Price rotary excavators (powered tunnelling machines) were used to bore the tunnels; these machines were ideally adapted for cutting through the stiff London clay. Temporary tracks were laid in the tunnels and small electric locomotives were used to carry away the excavated spoil. This was removed to the surface at the station shafts. Very little water-bearing soil was encountered, and only at Euston was any tunnel constructed in compressed air. This was because a layer of water-bearing sand was encountered (the Woolwich and Reading beds); a pressure of 15 psi (1.03 bar – about twice normal atmospheric pressure) was required to hold back the water. The tunnels continued to leak slightly, and a sump was installed to the north of Euston Road station to collect and remove the water. (The C&SLR had similar problems when they extended their line to Euston in 1907.) Compressed air working was also employed at Charing Cross to protect the main-line station by reducing the risk of any subsidence below the heavy structures.

When the Central London Railway was constructed in the 1890s, the stations were all placed on a slight hump, with the tracks arriving on a rising gradient of 1 in 60, and departing on a slope of 1 in 30. This had two advantages. Firstly it brought the platforms slightly closer to the surface, and so reduced the time taken to access them. Secondly, and more importantly, the gradients helped to slow arriving trains and accelerate departing trains, thus reducing wear on the brakes and usage of electricity. Where possible, tube railways constructed since have followed this principle. However, this was not done on the CCE&HR because of the overall gradient. Between the stations at Charing Cross and Hampstead there is a difference in elevation of 272 feet.

Facing page A rotary excavator at work under London. The rails in the foreground were for the wagons that took the excavated clay back to the nearest shaft for removal to the surface. The pistons that drove the tunnelling shield forwards into the clay can clearly be seen around the edge of the completed ring of cast iron tunnel lining.

At the Hampstead station shaft, work was suspended in late August 1903 because of the presence of underground springs filling the workings with water. A correspondent to *The Times* resurrected the idea of the Heath being ruined by the railway company draining off all the water. Some years later the local Scientific Society reported the discovery of at least five different species of fossil from the London clay during the tunnelling at the station.

By November the sites for ten of the stations had been purchased, and the cutting of the running tunnels was making good progress. Apart from the water-bearing ground at Euston the only other difficulties were under Hampstead Heath, where the pressure of up to 250ft of clay distorted and broke the tunnelling machine and led to the tunnels at this point having to be hand dug.

Between Golder's Green and Hampstead lay the site for another station, called North End, which was to have its building on the west side of Hampstead Way. The platform tunnels were constructed with the rest of the line, as were the subways and stairs leading to the lower lift landing, but no connection was made with the surface. A complication was that Hampstead Way was a new road, and the local planners kept adjusting its location as plans for housing changed. The main problem lay with Hampstead Heath, which had been protected from development since 1871. The housing that was planned for the vicinity of the station was opposed by the Hampstead Heath Extension Council (HHEC). One of their more prominent members was the social reformer Dame Henrietta Barnett, who had met Yerkes on a voyage to Europe in 1896, and discussed her plans for a garden suburb. Negotiations with one of the landowners, Eton College, for the purchase of the land started in 1903, when a price of £600 per acre was sought. The money proved harder to raise than expected, and so Eton dropped their price to £450 per acre, reckoning on the rest of their land increasing in value because of the proximity of the new part of the Heath. They also insisted on the construction of Wildwood Road and Hampstead Way.

The purchase went ahead in September 1904, with 80 acres of land that to this day forms the extension to the Heath, lying north-east of Golders Green station. The HHEC welcomed the construction of North End station, for it would enable Londoners to travel cheaply to the fresh air and open spaces. However, fears were raised that so many people walking to the Heath from the station would lead to erosion of the soil nearby. To answer these concerns the HHEC suggested that the railway company construct the station further to the north-west, where the tunnels ended (and in fact so close to the station at Golder's Green as to be completely unattractive from the company's perspective).

The creation of the Heath Extension and plans for day-trippers did not appeal to the CCE&HR though. Such visitors to the Heath would be nowhere near as lucrative as housing estates full of commuters, and so the station plans were scaled back. In 1906 the number of lifts was reduced from three to two, thus removing the need to construct one of the shafts at the station. Later in the year the plans for the station were scrapped altogether, leaving the Underground with its only station that was constructed but not opened.

At a Board meeting of 18th November 1907 it was decided to put aside the sum of £38,600 as contingency for completing the construction of the station at a later date. This included £15,500 for the tunnels and shafts, £10,000 for the building, and £8,000 for the lifts. In the years since it has become known to Underground staff as Bull & Bush, from the hostelry in the vicinity of the site for its building.

The junction at Camden Town was of mild concern to the BoT. It was the first time that a junction on a tube railway would see regular passenger service and they wanted to make sure that it was not possible for trains heading southbound to collide. They had originally insisted that overrun tunnels be built between the platforms and the junction, into which trains would be diverted if the route was not set for them. They were concerned when plans provided in August 1903 had these tunnels omitted, and insisted that the signalling be arranged such that a southbound train on the Highgate branch could not depart South Kentish Town station until any train in the southbound platform from Hampstead had cleared the junction.

This was not popular with the railway company, who realized it would restrict the flow of trains. As a compromise, they adjusted the platform stopping positions at Camden Town, placing them slightly further north to give a greater distance from the junction. The platforms were longer than the anticipated train length, so this posed no operational problems. Together with the fail-safe signalling that was installed, the company proved to the BoT that it was impossible for trains to collide, and so this was permitted.

A late addition to the line was a station at Mornington Crescent, which was authorized in the CCE&HR Act of 1904. The section between Euston and Camden Town was fairly long and the new station would serve the district south of Camden. In the same year the BoT raised objections to the layout of Oxford Street station. The position of the Central London Railway tunnels (at their station, confusingly called Tottenham Court Road) precluded much from being done, but the absence of any low-level subway connection between the two railways was considered to be a problem. Negotiations between the companies were put in hand, and the missing connection was finally put in place, saving passengers a tedious interchange via the ticket offices or even the street.

By March 1905 the lift shafts at 11 stations had been sunk, over 88 per cent of the running tunnels between Charing Cross and the tunnel portals at Golder's Green had been constructed, and 57 per cent of the Highgate branch. The station platform tunnels at seven stations (Leicester Square, Euston, Camden Town, Chalk Farm, Belsize Park, North End, and South Kentish Town, plus one tunnel at Kentish Town as well) were complete, with another seven stations in progress. Track laying was ready to start between Camden Town and Hampstead.

At Golder's Green the car-shed buildings were being erected. These comprised four brick buildings with pitched steel and glass roofs each 600 feet long. Erected by Messrs Bott and Stennett, they provided enough covered track (15 roads) to accommodate all of the cars for the line. Twelve roads had inspection pits allowing access to the underside of the trains. To the north of the buildings lay four more sidings, with another two sidings positioned between the depot and the station. Offices and storerooms were provided on the south side of the buildings.

The depot was well-equipped with tools to enable all of the necessary maintenance work to be undertaken on site. Two 10-ton travelling cranes ran above the machine shop; together they could be used to lift a car body from its bogies (the undercarriages that house the wheels and motors, on which the car bodies rest). A training school for drivers was built next to the machine shop, and was fitted with the electrical control gear from a train (without motors), and air-brake apparatus. This was used to demonstrate how the trains worked, and how to fix faults that might occur while out on service.

A sketch from the *Daily Graphic* showing the damage to the station and theatre (in the foreground).

The first task undertaken in the depot prior to opening was the assembly of the cars. The bodies, bogies, and electrical gear were supplied separately, and around 150 staff were employed in assembling these.

At Charing Cross the company faced a formidable engineering challenge. The original intention had been to place the station building on the north side of the Strand, but in late 1905 an agreement was reached with the South Eastern & Chatham Railway (SE&CR) to place the ticket hall under the forecourt of their main-line station. The difficulty was that the CCE&HR were forbidden from closing the forecourt in order to construct the station, as this would disrupt the cab traffic at the station. It was decided that the only way to proceed was to tunnel upwards from the running tunnels. As can be imagined, this would be arduous work – especially digging the lift shafts from the bottom up.

Fate intervened on 5th December 1905, at 15.40. A wrought iron tie-rod in the huge arched roof of the main-line station snapped, and the large glazed roof collapsed, killing six people, bringing down the wall on the southern side of the station, and badly damaging the adjacent Avenue Theatre. The station was closed until 19th March 1906. An enquiry in January showed that the tie rod had been flawed from the beginning, but in such a way that it was not obvious to the naked eye. Verdicts of accidental death were recorded.

Although a tragedy for those killed and injured, it presented an opportunity for the tube railway. They lost no time in arranging to open the forecourt, with an agreement being sealed with the SER on 2nd January 1906. This would enable the tube station to be constructed in the normal manner, top downwards. In the 3½ months that the station was closed, they sunk one lift shaft to its full depth of 73 feet and constructed the walls and roof of the ticket hall. The forecourt was reinstated, and then the second shaft was sunk from beneath, with the works at the station being completed by September 1906. In recognition of the many months of difficult work that they had avoided, the cost of rebuilding the main-line station was met in part by the CCE&HR.

A prospectus issued by the railway on 2nd March 1905 to raise another £800,000 from the sale of debenture stock provided a list of the stations on the line. The names were now given as Charing Cross, Cranbourn Street, Oxford Street, Tottenham Court Road (Goodge Street), Euston Road (Warren Street), Euston (Melton Street),

Mornington Crescent, Camden Town, Chalk Farm (Adelaide Road), Belsize, Hampstead (Heath Street), North End, Golder's Green, Castle Road, Kentish Town, Tufnell Park (Brecknock Road), and Highgate. The last four stations in the list were on the branch to Highgate (originally to be called Archway Tavern).

The Edgware & Hampstead Railway gained permission in their Act of 1905 to re-route their line at Golder's Green. Back in 1902 the line had been abandoned south-east to Hampstead to avoid duplicating the CCE&HR. This had left the two railways parallel but unconnected at Golder's Green; the authorized route of the E&HR effectively terminated on the other side of the new tube railway depot. The new route connected with the CCE&HR end-on, and rejoined the original route just west of Hoop Lane.

In 1906 a new agreement was reached with the Watford & Edgware Railway, which had received the Royal Assent three years before. The W&ER together with the CCE&HR and the UERL agreed that the double-track line to be constructed north of Golder's Green would be run separately from the tube railway, and passengers would have to change trains at the station. Rather than power being drawn from conductor rails (the method used on the tubes), the trains on the new line northwards would draw their power from overhead wires. Yerkes wrote to the BoT in May 1904 to ask if they would have any objections to this; after some thought they decided not. However, a year later the company decided that conventional tube trains would be used after all.

Attempts to extend the time permitted by Parliament to purchase the required land were made in 1907, as well as a proposal for amalgamation with the Edgware & Hampstead Railway. These were unsuccessful, but in 1909 the Bills for the two railways were successfully passed, allowing both an additional two years to purchase land and start construction. In the following years no progress was made with either, and the W&ER company remained in independent existence until 1922, when it was bought up by the UERL. It was finally wound up in 1934.

The physical construction of the railway was only one part of the work that was going on. Other activities included designing the layout of the stations and signals, negotiating agreements with other railway companies, arranging the contracts, and drafting the by-laws. The latter were completed and submitted to the BoT on 12th April 1907, and received approval four days later. They were identical to those used on the Baker Street & Waterloo, and Great Northern, Piccadilly & Brompton Railways — not very surprising, given their common ownership, and the fact that like most railways they based the by-laws on model clauses from the BoT. Fines for transgression were mostly set at a maximum of 40 shillings for a first offence (rising to £5 for subsequent occurrences). Bringing firearms, explosives, or inflammable substances onto the railway, or vandalizing its property would incur a fine up to £5.

Similarly, a rule book was required for the railway's staff. The Baker Street & Waterloo, and the Great Northern, Piccadilly & Brompton had been issued with their own (very similar) rule books upon opening. This was not the case with the Hampstead Tube; instead, a combined rule book for all three tube railways was issued on 1st June 1907.

The tunnelling was completed in April 1906, but work to lay the tracks and cables had started earlier as the tunnels were finished. The signalling had to be fitted and tested; stations built and lifts installed; staff trained. All in all, 1906 was a very busy year for the company, but at last their railway was getting into shape for the public.

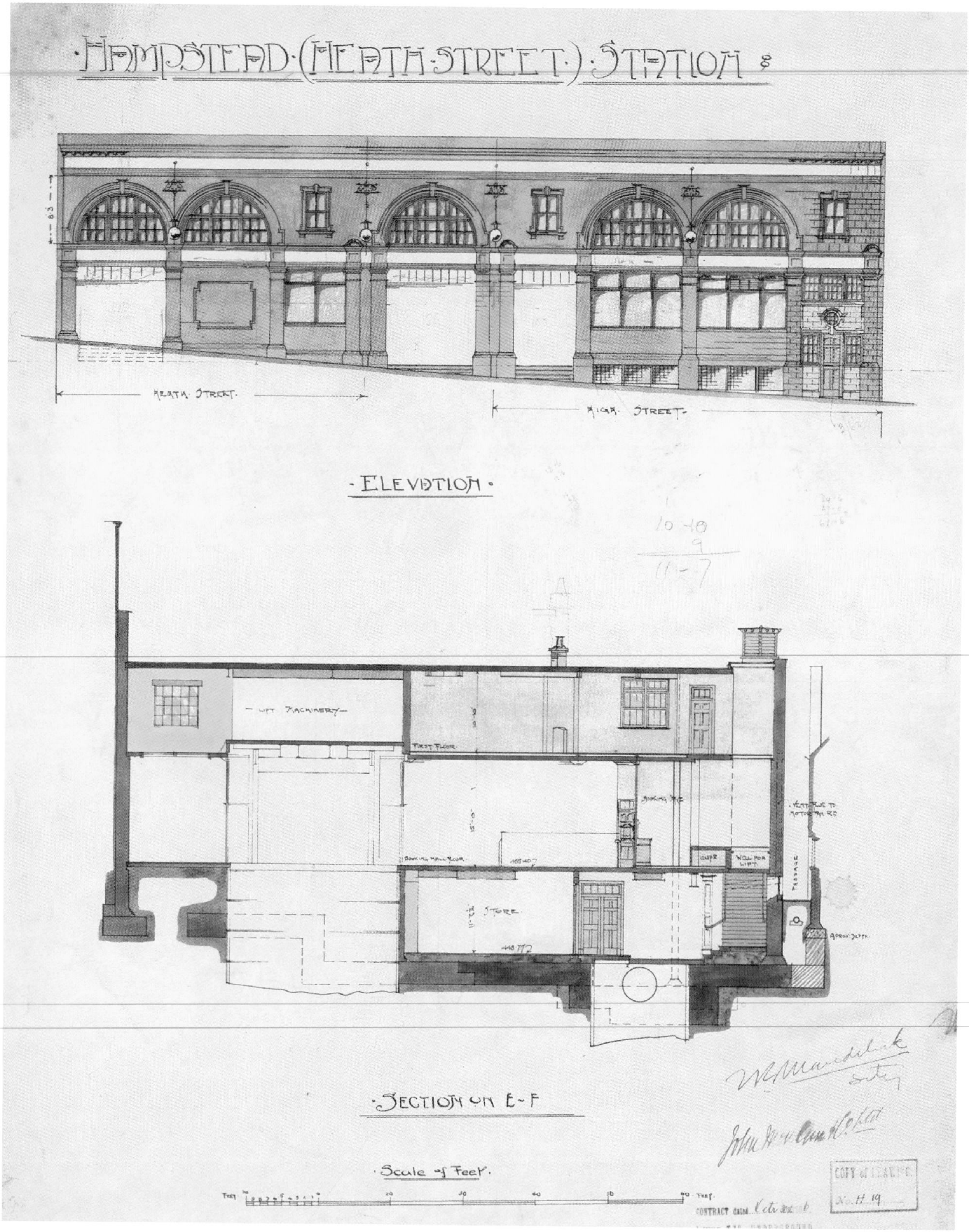

·HAMPSTEAD·(HEATH·STREET·)·STATION·

HEATH STREET

HIGH STREET

·ELEVATION·

LIFT MACHINERY

FIRST FLOOR

BOOKING OFFICE

VENTILATOR TO METROPOLITAN RD

BOOKING HALL FLOOR

SHAFT

WELL FOR LIFT

STORE

APRON PATH

·SECTION ON E-F·

·Scale of Feet·

24

THE STATIONS

The stations on the line were all constructed and finished in the UERL Art Nouveau style that people had seen on the Bakerloo and Piccadilly tubes. They were designed by Leslie Green, who had been appointed in 1903 as the architect to the UERL. With the exception of Golder's Green (described below) the buildings were built using steel frames, with walls of brick. On most outside-facing surfaces these were clad in glazed terracotta blocks, made in a colour described as 'ox-blood' by the Leeds Fireclay Company. This finish was selected as the result of a competition between various manufacturers, which had involved the erection of full-size models. The buildings were two storeys high, incorporating lift machine rooms on the first floor. The steel frames allowed the addition of extra storeys above at a future date, which would provide rental income to the company. Separate entrances and exits were provided, with large arched windows in the façade above. A frieze at roof level contained the station name in large black letters on a white tiled background; a similar frieze between the ground and first floors gave the company name. This was generally given as HAMPSTEAD TUBE, although Mornington Crescent, Belsize Park, and Highgate had space for HAMPSTEAD TUBE RAILWAY, and Leicester Square used PICCADILLY AND HAMPSTEAD TUBE RAILWAYS.

One other interesting feature at Leicester Square station, and still extant today, relates to one of the original tenants. Wisden, the cricket company, had occupied one of the offices in the building, and when the site was purchased for the station moved to a replacement office on Newport Street, behind and adjoining the station. Access to this office was arranged via a passageway from Cranbourn Street, and a terracotta frieze incorporating Wisden's name together with a ball, a set of stumps, and two cricket bats was provided over the entrance.

There were three stations on the line that differed from the standard 'house' style described above. Charing Cross and Oxford Street (now Tottenham Court Road) stations had subsurface ticket halls, and buildings were never provided. Stairwells led from street level down into them. The machine rooms for the lifts were located in chambers at the bottom of the shafts, there being no headroom to accommodate these in the normal position. Golder's Green was the only station with a surface platform, and for reasons never adequately explained did not appear to be designed by Green. London Underground have suggested that the building might have been designed by the architect to the District Railway, Harry Ford; it is also possible that it was designed by the builders, Bott & Stennett. It had a simple red brick building, with no glazed terracotta, and the general style was unlike any of the other stations. The railway name was placed onto the front of a metal canopy, with the station name appearing on the sides.

Facing page Elevation and a section of Hampstead station, the latter showing the basement and foundations.

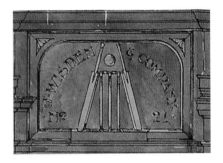

The terracotta tile at Leicester Square recalls the time when the cricket publishers Wisden were tenants in offices here.

An early (c.1909) view of Heath Street in Hampstead, showing the station on the right.

Facing page upper The original terminus of the eastern branch, today called Archway, shortly after opening, with a large number of maps and posters for the line on display.

Facing page lower The original ticket office at Golder's Green station, shown in 1912. Some features, such as the tiling and the clock are similar to other Hampstead Tube stations, but the overall style is unlike any other UERL station.

The entrance to the CCE&HR and C&SLR stations at Euston in 1915. The word 'TUBE' has been painted over after falling out of favour (see page 38). Public lavatories were provided at stations other than Charing Cross, Oxford Street, Tottenham Court Road (now Goodge Street), Camden Town, and Tufnell Park.

Inside, the ticket halls had green glazed tiles up to shoulder height, with a decorative frieze at the top. The floors were laid in mauve mosaic, and ticket office windows were either moulded ceramic or wood.

The upper lift landing doors and their surrounds were made from teak. Otis, an American company that had developed lift technology over the previous fifty years, supplied the lifts. The company was quick to point out that the entire equipment of the lift cars was made of steel, except for the floors, which used fireproof wood. The electric lifts were mostly placed in pairs in shafts 23 feet in diameter. The lift cars were trapezoid in shape, and accommodated up to about 70 passengers (although the practical maximum might well have been lower), moving them at up to 200 feet per minute at most stations, although Hampstead might have been slightly faster. Separate gates for entrance and exit from the lifts were provided, increasing the throughput of the lifts and reducing conflicting passenger flows; the entrance gates were manually opened and closed by the liftman, but the exit gates were air-operated. Separate passageways were used for those accessing and leaving the platforms to maintain the separate flows.

At Leicester Square the lifts served both the Piccadilly and Hampstead tubes, and the lower lift landing was at a level between the two railways. This station also had one lift in a shaft 16 feet in diameter. Hampstead had three shafts with five lifts, because the great depth of the platforms meant that the wait for a lift would otherwise be too long; there would otherwise have been no justification for this lavish provision of equipment. At Euston, Camden Town, Belsize Park, Hampstead, and Highgate there were shafts containing one lift with space for another if the traffic demanded. Mornington Crescent, Chalk Farm, South Kentish Town, Kentish Town, and Tufnell Park all had spare shafts with provision for an additional pair of lifts. A spiral staircase was provided at all underground stations, usually in a separate shaft 16 feet in diameter. The variations were at Charing Cross and Euston, where the stairs occupied half a standard lift shaft. The latter station was constructed with two entrances: one at Melton Street, where a conventional station building was provided, and one into the main-line station. It was the latter entrance that had the stairs and lift in a single shaft, as well as a second shaft with two lifts. The stairs at Oxford Street were not ready for opening on 22nd June 1907, due to leakage from a sewer. The Board of Trade allowed the station to open though, as an alternative exit was available via the CLR station.

At Golder's Green the platforms were built on an embankment at roughly first floor level. Two subways led back from the ticket hall, running perpendicular to the platforms, and stairways led from these up to the platforms.

Low-level connections were provided at some of the stations where interchange with other tube railways was possible. At Leicester Square this was fairly straightforward, as both lines were owned by the same company and through fares were provided from the outset. As mentioned earlier, the layout at Oxford Street allowed passengers to change to the Tottenham Court Road station of the Central London Railway, and a ticket office was provided at low level. A similar situation existed at Euston with the City & South London Railway.

At Charing Cross the main entrance to the station was in the western corner of the station forecourt. The exit led out onto Villiers Street, and a third connection was made directly into the main-line station, allowing interchange without going outside. These arrangements were criticized by the Board of Trade when the line was inspected. They noted that Villiers Street would make a far better entrance, as it was more conveniently situated for passengers arriving from the District station at the other end of the street. However, it transpired that the main-line company had (for some reason) forbidden an entrance from being made there. The CCE&HR directors had had some kind of falling out with the main-line company, and were reluctant to ask for a change, so instead they did the simplest thing they could: they ignored the problem and let the public do what they wished. The BoT seemed to be quite happy with this as a solution.

The platforms were the part of the stations that attracted the most attention. Instead of the uniform white tiling found on previous tube railways, each was decorated with a coloured pattern. Although no definite reason has been found, it has been suggested that the colours and patterns were an aid to recognition in a time when adult literacy was not as great as it is today. The tiles were all 9 × 3ins and were supplied by several firms. Each platform featured the name of the station three times, at each end and in the centre, fired into the tiles in brown lettering five tiles high. The pattern featured on the end walls and between the name panels. The panels were divided into sections by tiled bands that rose from platform level and wrapped around the tunnel ceiling to the trackside wall. At most stations the bands and the pattern were in the same colour, with either cream or white tiles used as background. Art Nouveau 'Way Out' and 'No Exit' signs were included in the tilework adjacent to the passageways on most stations south of Camden Town. On the trackside wall opposite the passageways leading onto the platforms, tiled signs indicating the direction and destination of the line were provided. The only complete examples of these signs to remain on a Hampstead Tube station are on the northbound Highgate branch platform at Camden Town and the southbound platform at Kentish Town.

Rather unusually, when considered in today's safety-conscious age, bookstalls were provided on the platforms at many (if not all) of the stations. This caused some concern at the headquarters of the London Fire Brigade (LFB), who objected to the danger of storing quantities of paper below ground. When contacted by the BoT, the railway company pointed out in a rather blasé manner that 'it is the invariable practice of Railway Companies to have these bookstalls on platforms'. The Central London Railway had bookstalls, and was used by the CCE&HR as the precedent. (The BoT fire prevention regulations had been drawn up after the CLR opened, and so did not apply.) After some discussion between the parties the bookstalls were retained, being 'much used and appreciated by the travelling public'. No matches or tobacco products were sold, although the LFB feared that this was only a matter of time.

The subways connecting the platforms with the lift landings, and some of the spiral staircases were also decorated using tiles in the same colours as on the platforms, although without the decorative patterns. The exception, once again, was Golder's Green, where a diamond pattern was used on the sides of the staircases.

The platforms were illuminated by electric arc lamps, which were fed from the lift circuits. If this supply failed then they could be switched to the traction current supply. Incandescent lamps were also provided, powered from the local electricity company. Every precaution was taken against the possibility of the station being plunged into darkness.

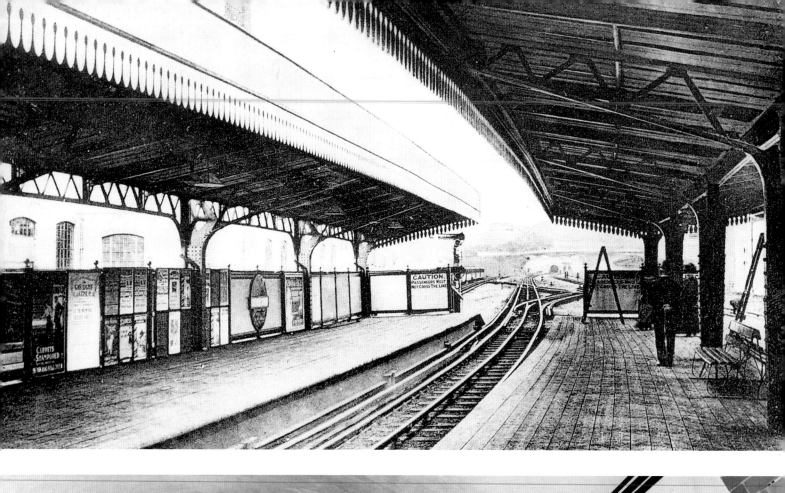

Many of the stations opened with names that differed from those originally proposed. The station in Camden was originally to have been called Hampstead Road, suggesting a location in the vicinity of Mornington Crescent. It was later changed to Camden (Mother Redcap) after a local hostelry before construction and when the site was moved northwards. As already noted, the station at Mornington Crescent was added in the CCE&HR Act of 1904. The northern terminus of Hampstead was called Heath Street until very near the opening day, and it is the latter name that was fired onto the tiles of the platforms, still visible today on both platform walls.

The stations of the CCE&HR are all broadly similar. They have two platforms in separate tunnels, with the platforms generally situated between the tracks so that common staircases serve both. These lead up to the lower lift landings. Most pairs of platforms are thus at the same level, but those at Kentish Town and Tufnell Park are at different depths and are all on the east side of the tracks. For undocumented reasons the tunnels switch position either side of Kentish Town, and therefore this station has right-hand running. Camden Town has four platforms, two on each branch. In order to keep the junctions on separate levels both southbound platforms are situated at a lower level than the northbound platforms.

Golder's Green had a more spacious layout at opening, with three platforms and two tracks. The central platform was for departures, allowing passengers to board trains at either side. The two side platforms handled arriving passengers. The platforms were situated to the south of the depot. Beyond the station the tracks continued to a point near the Finchley Road, indicating the direction in which the company hoped to extend. These were used for stabling cars when required.

Crossovers were constructed at key points along the route, allowing trains to be reversed. Scissor crossovers were provided south of Highgate and Golder's Green, and north of Charing Cross, allowing trains to terminate in either platform. Trailing crossovers were installed to the north of Hampstead and Mornington Crescent stations, allowing trains to be turned short if required.

Within the tunnels the track was at standard gauge, and laid on sleepers made from fireproof Australian Karri wood (a type of eucalyptus). Felt pads were used between the sleepers and the cast-iron chairs holding the rails, as this helped to reduce noise and vibration, as well as ensuring a better fit. The sleepers had their middle thirds supported on a bed of concrete in the invert of the tunnels, and the space under each end (and between the sleepers) was filled with crushed granite chippings. The engineers felt that this type of support, previously used on the Piccadilly Tube, would make the permanent way more flexible, and so provide a better ride. The running rails were all (like so much of the equipment) imported from the USA — in this case from the steel town of Pittsburgh.

Lamps were provided throughout the running tunnels, spaced at 42ft intervals, and fed from a dedicated electricity supply at 220 V. They were, at least for the first months of operation, permanently lit. To increase the effectiveness of the lighting the insides of the tunnels were whitewashed, although it can be imagined that they rapidly became coated in dust and dirt.

A train running a trial service prior to opening. It is passing southbound through the crossover tunnel immediately north of Hampstead station, over 200 feet below the surface.

Facing page upper The station at Golder's Green around the time of opening, with the mouths of the tunnels in the background. At the end of the wooden platform on the left is a semaphore signal. On the extreme left are the buildings of Golder's Green depot.

Facing page lower A typical tube platform on the Hampstead Tube in 1907. The tiled pattern and name can be seen along with the tiled rings over the ceiling. Trains consisting of three, four, or five cars were to stop with their cabs alongside the '3, 4 & 5' sign; six car trains would stop at the tunnel mouth.

EARLY YEARS

Services on the railway were provided by 150 new cars constructed by the American Car & Foundry Company of America. Some of the construction work was carried out in Manchester, but the American influence has led to the term 'car' being used on the London Underground to this day. It was alleged by the UERL at the time that no British manufacturer had sufficient experience with the techniques necessary to make the steel shells.

The cars were transferred from Manchester to London via the Midland Railway, before being delivered one at a time on horse-drawn trailers to Golder's Green depot where their assembly was completed. A gantry alongside No. 1 road in the depot was used to offload them. Sixty of the cars were each equipped with two 200 h.p. (150 KW) motors, with the remainder being trailers. Fifty of these trailers were provided with driving controls and termed 'control trailers'. Soon after opening, ten of the remaining trailers were converted into control trailers.

As to be expected, the cars were very similar to those on the Bakerloo and Piccadilly tubes. They were 50ft long and 8ft 6¾ins wide at the waist. The motor cars had a full-width cab at one end, with an equipment compartment for the electrical control gear directly behind. This took up 12ft of the length of the cars, and was positioned above the motor bogies. These had larger wheels than the trailer bogies, giving a characteristic raised section of the car frame at this point, above which were ventilation grilles.

Where exactly this might be in Golder's Green is not known, but such unspoilt countryside was short lived once the railway arrived.

Left One of the original motor cars for the railway, showing the gate end at the left, and the driving cab to the right. The equipment compartment is behind the louvred grilles.

Facing page upper The station at Belsize Park was unique in having a forecourt garden. This was forced upon the company by the LCC, who insisted that the building be set back from the road.

Facing page lower The station at Golder's Green shortly after opening. The building is unlike any other on the Hampstead Tube.

The trailing ends of the motor cars were fitted with an open platform protected by metal lattice gates, opening to the sides for passenger access, and also to the adjacent car to allow for passengers to pass between cars in an emergency. The trailer cars had similar gated platforms at both ends, with the controlling equipment mounted on one platform of the control trailers.

The gates were operated by gatemen, who manned each adjacent pair of gates, and also announced the names of the stations to the passengers within each car. The passengers were provided with 42 seats in the motor cars and 52 in the trailers. These were covered in non-flammable rattan, and fitted with decorative armrests. Leather straps hung from the ceiling in two rows for the benefit of those without a seat. Fire-resistant mahogany veneer was used for interior panelling. Smoking accommodation was to be found in the motor cars, and labels on the windows indicated this; trailers were all non-smoking.

The dimensions varied very slightly between the three tube lines. The Bakerloo had smaller motor compartments (which caused problems), and the Piccadilly cars were manufactured in France and Hungary. The Hampstead cars had a different type of brake block from the others (to reduce metallic dust in the tunnels), and were also fitted with sprung buffing plates between the cars to minimize bumping.

The exterior of the cars was painted in a dark red livery (known as 'lake'), with gold used for the car number, the initials of the company, and the lining. Plates mounted on the car sides and in the right-hand front window indicated the destination of the train. These read GOLDERS GREEN, HAMPSTEAD, HIGHGATE, or CHARING + in white on black.

The British Thomson-Houston Company supplied the motors. Control was on the multiple-unit system, whereby a single driver could control motors along the length of the train without the need for heavy power cables between the cars. Instead, low-voltage control circuits were provided that operated the traction circuits on the motor cars. This system had been first used in London by the Central London Railway, who had converted all of their trains to multiple-unit operation in 1903. Steel collector shoes were fitted to both bogies on the motor cars to make contact with the conductor rails.

Westinghouse air brakes were provided on the trains. Unlike the CLR, which had two men in each cab, the Yerkes trains had a deadman's handle device on the controller, which would cause the brakes to be applied and the motor current cut if the driver became incapacitated.

The signalling on the railway was identical to that provided on the other Yerkes tubes. Track circuits, powered by low-voltage direct current, were provided via the running rails, which detected the presence of trains and operated automatic signals. Signalmen in cabins at Charing Cross, Mornington Crescent, Camden Town, Hampstead, Golder's Green, and Highgate controlled the semi-automatic signals at the junctions and crossovers. Illuminated track diagrams were provided in the cabins, showing the location of all trains in the area. The sections on each diagram were normally back-lit, except when a train was present. The dark sections indicated the presence of a train. The cabins had signal frames supplied by Westinghouse.

One interesting and unusual feature came about from the line being the first to have a junction used in passenger service. At Mornington Crescent station, drivers of northbound trains were required to operate a plunger confirming their destination to the signalman at Camden Town, who would then set the points appropriately.

The tunnel signals were illuminated by oil lamps and consisted of a plate with red and green glass that was raised and lowered pneumatically. The open section of line at Golder's Green featured the semaphore signals standard on main-line railways, which were also operated pneumatically.

All signals were (and still are) accompanied by electro-pneumatically operated trainstops. These are small levers placed to the right of the right-hand running rail that rise up when the signal is at danger, and activate the brakes on any train that attempts to pass by hitting a lever on the train called the tripcock. This safety system was piloted on the Ealing & South Harrow Railway, which was owned by the Metropolitan District Railway, and proved to be so successful that it is still in use on most London Underground lines today.

The electricity for the railway was supplied by the UERL power station constructed at Lots Road in Chelsea. This site was originally chosen for the GNP&BR, and subsequently the specification for the equipment was increased allowing it to power all of the UERL railways. The output was 11,000 volts at a frequency of 33 Hz. This was distributed first to Earl's Court (the closest station to the power station), and then on to a network of substations, which transformed it to the various different voltages required by railway systems.

The Hampstead Tube made use of five substations. Four were new, and were sited at Golder's Green, Belsize Park, Kentish Town, and Euston. Belsize Park was equipped with a pair of 1.2 KW rotary converters; the other three each had a pair of 800 KW rotary converters. The fifth substation was at Charing Cross, and already supplied the District and Bakerloo Railways. It was located beneath the Victoria Embankment Gardens, and was equipped with four 1.5 KW converters. The high-voltage cables descended a shaft at Charing Cross substation and entered the cable subway under Villiers Street. This linked to the space under the northbound platform at Charing Cross station, and then on to the northbound running tunnels. The cables were supported by brackets fitted on the tunnel lining to the other substations, which were all constructed adjacent to their respective stations.

The traction current was supplied to the trains on the same system adopted by all of the other railways in the Yerkes combine, namely conductor shoes on the train rubbing along two conductor rails. One rail was located centrally between the running rails, and 1½ins above them; the other 1ft 4ins outside the running rails, and 3ins above. The height difference prevented the collector shoes from coming into contact with the running rails at junctions. The use of two conductor rails, providing an insulated return circuit for the traction current, was chosen for two reasons. Firstly the company wanted to prevent current leaking to earth, and causing possible electrolytic corrosion of the cast-iron tunnel lining, gas pipes, and any other metallic subsurface items, and secondly to prevent interference with the direct current track circuits that operated the signalling via the running rails. On the Hampstead Tube the centre rail was negative, and the outer rail positive, with the traction supply being provided at 550 V DC. They were both mounted on porcelain insulators made by Doulton (who are more commonly known for their tableware, but made electrical insulators from the 1840s onwards).

A pair of bare wires mounted on small insulators was carried along the side of the tunnels. In the event of an emergency, drivers could clip fly-leads from a telephone mounted in his cab onto these wires and communicate with the next station. Staff at the station could then arrange for appropriate action to be taken, for example, contacting the substation to remove the traction current. (About 20 years later the system was modified so that the wires could be pinched together, causing the traction current to be switched off automatically. The telephone handset was then used to talk to an attendant in the nearest substation.)

A separate feed of electricity was provided to the lifts at the stations, at 575 V, from the nearest substation. The substations also supplied the low-voltage track circuits, the tunnel lighting, some station lighting, and generated the compressed air used by the trainstops and signals.

The departure of a train was an elaborate ritual. Each gateman was responsible for closing the gates on the cars either side of his position. When the rear gates were closed, this gateman rang a bell that sounded beside the next man along; this bell signal was passed along the train to the guard, who rode between the first and second cars. He then rang a bell for the driver, upon which the train could leave.

From its opening a 2-minute service was operated between Charing Cross and Camden Town on weekdays during the peak hours, reducing slightly to every 2½ minutes off peak. Here the service split equally, providing a 4-minute peak and 5-minute off-peak service to Highgate and Hampstead. However, only one train in three continued beyond the latter station to Golder's Green, as the passenger demand was not yet there. This explains why a crossover was provided only one station away from the end of the branch.

The Sunday service was slightly less frequent, but still provided a train every three minutes between Charing Cross and Camden Town.

A table in the opening brochure for the line showed that the first trains departed each of the termini at 05.17 on weekdays, and around 07.30 on Sundays. The last trains departed at about 00.30 (except Golder's Green, which was 00.15) on weekdays, and 23.30 on Sundays.

From Sunday 28th July 1907 a bus service was provided between Golder's Green and Hendon, for which through tickets could be purchased with the railway. This was operated by Birch Brothers on behalf of the railway, and used new motor buses operating a 12-minute service in the peaks, and 24 minutes at other times. Unfortunately the buses proved unreliable and were replaced from 1st December by a horse-bus service running at 15-minute intervals.

Another service for which through ticketing was available was to St Albans via Finchley, which was operated at weekends and holidays.

The original intention had been to operate 6-car trains, with a motor car at each end and control trailers in the central positions, allowing the trains to be divided into 3-car units (comprising motor car, trailer, control trailer) for off-peak services. By the time they were delivered, experience on the Bakerloo and Piccadilly tubes had shown the passenger forecasts to be very optimistic, and 5-car trains were used instead. The conversion of ten trailers into control trailers allowed the trains to be formed with two control trailers and one trailer between motor cars. This allowed all thirty trains to be uncoupled into 2- and 3-car units for off-peak services.

Fares were based on distance travelled (except for the early-morning workmen's tickets), and the accompanying table from the opening brochure provides more detail. Season tickets were also sold, and over 1,000 were purchased in the first week alone. It was also possible to purchase through tickets to the Piccadilly Railway (interchange at Leicester Square), the C&SLR (at Euston), and the London & North Western mainline (also at Euston) from around the time of opening.

HAMPSTEAD TUBE

(Charing Cross, Euston, and Hampstead Railway)

Table of Single Local Fares

Station	Golder's Green	Hampstead	Belsize Park	Chalk Farm	Highgate	Tufnell Park	Kentish Town	South Kentish Town	Camden Town	Mornington Crescent	Euston	Euston Road	Tottenham Court Road	Oxford Street	Leicester Square	Charing Cross
Hampstead	D.1	*Hampstead.*														
Belsize Park	2	D.1	*Belsize Park.*													
Chalk Farm	2	1½	D.1	*Chalk Farm.*												
Highgate	3	2	2	D.2	*Highgate.*											
Tufnell Park	2	2	2	2	D.1	*Tufnell Park.*										
Kentish Town	2	2	2	2	1	D.1	*Kentish Town.*									
South Kentish Town	2	2	2	2	1	1	D.1	*South Kentish Town.*								
Camden Town	2	2	1	1	1½	1	1	D.1	*Camden Town.*							
Mornington Crescent	3	2	1½	1	2	1½	1	1	D.1	*Mornington Crescent.*						
Euston	3	2	2	1	2	2	1½	1	1	D.1	*Euston.*					
Euston Road	3	3	2	1½	2	2	1½	1½	1	1	D.1	*Euston Road.*				
Tottenham Court Road	3	3	2	2	2	2	2	1½	1½	1	1	D.1	*Tottenham Court Road.*			
Oxford Street	3	3	2	2	2	2	2	2	1½	1½	1½	1	D.1	*Oxford Street.*		
Leicester Square	3	3	3	2	3	3	2	2	2	2	2	1	1	D.1	*Leicester Square.*	
Charing Cross	3	3	3	2	3	3	2	2	2	2	2	1½	1	1	D.1	

WORKMEN'S FARES—1d. Any Distance, **2**d. Return.   Outward Journey to be completed by **8** a.m.

Johnson, Riddle & Co., Ltd., Printers, London.

The fare table included in the opening brochure for the railway.

By September 1907 the gatemen of the CCE&HR had drawn the censure of the *Railway Magazine*, which the previous year had been appalled by the Baker Street & Waterloo Railway formally adopting its 'Bakerloo' nickname. This year, it was the pronunciation of the Hampstead Tube staff that was concerning the magazine, which noted that

> After over 30 years of compulsory education, it must be humiliating to those responsible for teaching Cockneys, to find that the aspirate is conspicuous by its absence. Such is notably the case on the Charing Cross, Euston and Hampstead Railway. All day long, at every station, one hears the conductors of every other down train reiterate, "'Ampstead train; 'urry up, please." This is alternated by the chant of conductors on the other down trains, who exclaim "'Ighgate train; 'urry up, please." Perhaps, when the [CCE&HR] is appointing new conductors, candidates may be examined on the proper use of the aspirate.

Two months later, the *Railway Magazine* was pleased to note that the Traffic Assistant of the Hampstead Tube had taken decisive action. A traffic circular had been sent to the train staff reminding them of the need to pronounce station names both clearly and correctly, as laid down in Rules 78 and 79 of the Company.

37

Up to this point an apostrophe has been included in the name of Golders Green, consistent with the usage of the time. However, its use rapidly fell out of favour after the station opened, and from this point onwards the modern spelling of the name will be used.

The various operators of underground railways in London rapidly realized that they had far more to gain by co-operating, and presenting a co-ordinated front to the public, than by demonstrating the type of rivalry that had been seen between the early bus operators. The financial situation that many found themselves in meant the reductions in fares that competition would inevitably bring might lead to a desperate situation.

Sir George Gibb, who was now the Managing Director of the UERL, took decisive action, and arranged a meeting to be attended by representatives of his company, the Metropolitan Railway, the CLR, the C&SLR, the Great Northern & City Railway, and four of the major bus companies. This, the London Passenger Traffic Conference (LPTC), took place on 22nd July 1907, and agreed voting powers. One week later a further meeting was held, with a few additional parties, and they tentatively started the process of working together. By the end of the year the first adjustments in fares were being made, although these had little effect on the Hampstead Tube. The LPTC had become a regular meeting.

Albert Stanley was the new General Manager of the UERL. He made a suggestion that gave the system the name that it still bears today. His proposal was for the underground railway companies to adopt the common advertising name of UNDERGROUND. The new name would appear on stations and publicity in place of the individual company names, and would be displayed in white on blue. The station signs would show the name running vertically, and to see the effect of these the UERL mocked up the signs on photographs of their stations, using correction fluid and ink. White-on-blue tiled signs reading 'UNDERGROUND' were placed over the entrance to most stations over the next few years, irrespective of the wording that was there previously. Many of the friezes spelling out the company name on the station exteriors had the word TUBE removed at about the same time, and were amended to read HAMPSTEAD RAILWAY.

Another effect of this co-ordination was that maps now started to show all of the Underground lines, using different colours to distinguish them. Previously each company issued its own maps, which tended to highlight their services and show all other lines in an undifferentiated manner. The maps that were issued officially by the UERL adopted purple for the Hampstead Tube, although the exact colour seems to have varied from a light, lilac shade through to a dark maroon. It was also decided that the key to the maps would show the official name for each railway, although in 1908 these were sensibly shortened to the less cumbersome names that were in semi-official use.

A final, and very rational, pair of changes concerned station names. The odd situation whereby Oxford Street station on the Hampstead Tube afforded interchange with Tottenham Court Road station on the CLR was removed from 9th March 1908, when the CCE&HR station name was changed to match the CLR (although it appears that Oxford Street was retained as a suffix on the platform signs for some years). This forced the station to the north, originally opened as Tottenham Court Road, to be simultaneously renamed to Goodge Street. Later in the year, on 7th June, Euston Road became Warren Street, to avoid confusion with Euston station.

A commercial postcard from around 1909 showing Tufnell Park station. Unfortunately the card bears no caption, but it appears to show a school party, who have perhaps just travelled on the Underground for the first time.

A Hampstead correspondent to *The Times*, quoted in a leaflet dated 20th July 1907, wrote:

> The people who live on the upper slopes of this northern height are naturally the greatest gainers, though some of the more sensitive imaginations in our highly artistic community still shudder at the idea of descending nearly 200 feet into the bowels of the earth before they reach the station. These folks are not numerous enough to maintain omnibuses in competition with the burrowing trains. The old omnibus service from High Street, Hampstead, to St Giles's Church died a sudden death a few days after the tube was opened ... A passenger can now book through by the Hampstead and South London Tubes, changing from one to the other at Euston. The idea of reaching the Oval in 35 minutes from the upper parts of Hampstead seems almost too good to be true; but that is the promise of the timetable.

Tickets allowing travel to stations on the Piccadilly Tube, the C&SLR, and the London & North Western Railway were available from early on in the history of the CCE&HR. Both the railway companies and the public rapidly perceived the value of such arrangements, and within a short time additional through bookings had been made possible, courtesy of the LPTC.

Tickets allowing Hampstead Tube passengers access to the Bakerloo were available by 9th August 1907; with the CLR from 1st September 1907 (allowing the closure of the low-level ticket office at Tottenham Court Road); with the District (via the street at Charing Cross) from 1st July 1908; and with the GN&CR from 24th July 1908 (with passengers having to travel to Old Street via Euston on the C&SLR).

A further change in 1908 was the discontinuance of season tickets, which were withdrawn across the Yerkes tubes, and replaced with rolls or strips of six tickets. These could be purchased at a discount that made their cost similar to a season ticket for someone who made the same journey six days a week. The reasons given for abolishing season tickets were reported in *The Times* of 8th September as being low take-up (only 3 per cent of travellers using them), fraudulent usage, and (bizarrely) that

> It is found impracticable, because of the irritation aroused, to make every season ticket holder show his ticket every time he passes a ticket barrier, and it is impossible for every ticket-collector to know every season ticket holder by sight.

HAMPSTEAD RAILWAY
NON-STOP SERVICES
GOLDERS GREEN AND CHARING CROSS IN 16 MINS.

TRAINS LEAVE GOLDERS GREEN		TRAINS LEAVE CHARING CROSS	
WEEKDAYS	SATURDAYS ONLY	MONDAYS TO FRIDAYS	SATURDAYS
8 11	12 48	5 27	1 5
8 53	1 36	6 9	1 53
9 38	2 18	6 51	2 35
10 20	3 0	7 33	3 17
Hampstead 3 mins. later.		Tottenham Court Road 2½ mins. later.	

The non-stop trains were only possible because of the greater intervals between the regular stopping trains than exist today. They generally only saved five or six minutes on the complete journey. Most of this was gained on the branches north of Camden Town, where the train interval was double that on the line to the south. One passenger recollected waiting for ten minutes at Tottenham Court Road for the arrival of the theatre train, this interval allowing it to run without interruption to Hampstead.

This reasoning was disparaged by an irate season ticket holder in a letter to *The Times*:

It is perfectly ridiculous to suggest that there ever has been the slightest inconvenience attaching to season tickets, and to withdraw them in favour of tickets in strips of six is even more absurd. ...Who wants to be put to the bother of buying strips of tickets every week, and go about town with his pockets bulging out with them like a stuffed turkey?

The writer went on to claim that if few tickets were sold it was because the company did not advertise them, and made purchasing them as difficult as possible.

In July 1909 the managers attending the London Passenger Traffic Conference agreed that all stations selling tickets to Golders Green would also issue tickets to Hendon by bus, at the same 1d supplement that the Hampstead Tube charged.

Soon after the opening of the Yerkes tubes it was found that not all of the stations were equally patronized. Some had been built in areas that were less desirable to the commuting classes, and some were too close together. Three lifts were moved between stations in order to match capacity to demand. Warren Street had one lift removed, and Goodge Street lost two. These provided an extra lift at each of Tufnell Park, Kentish Town, and Belsize Park.

It was also realized that the service frequency could be increased if some trains omitted certain lightly used stations. Some minor changes were made to the signalling at the termini at the same time to improve the speed with which trains were reversed.

The first non-stop train ran on the Hampstead Tube in July 1908, it being the 07.59 departure from Highgate, which omitted all intermediate stations to Camden Town and took 4½ minutes to cover the 1¾ miles. Another non-stop service was introduced three months later, leaving Highgate at 08.49. These services were amended in November, the first having an additional stop at Tufnell Park, and the second calling at Kentish Town.

The Golders Green branch gained its first non-stop services in September 1909, with seven trains each day (three southbound in the morning, and four northbound in the evening) running direct from Euston to Golders Green, shaving 2½ minutes off the journey time. A large board was mounted on the centre of the leading car pronouncing the non-stop status of the train – presumably for the benefit of those waiting at stations that were being omitted.

The following month an extra non-stop train was added, and the connecting three-horse omnibuses to Hendon were arranged to run an express service as well. By 1911 Hampstead had been added as an additional stop.

Theatre trains, pioneered on the Piccadilly, were introduced from October 1910, departing Golders Green at 19.16, calling at Hampstead, and then running non-stop to Tottenham Court Road. The corresponding return service left at 23.15. By 1913 a similar service had been added to and from Highgate.

Non-stopping proved to be such a success that from July 1913 it was introduced all day. The general pattern was that the quieter stations (namely South Kentish Town, and Chalk Farm to Goodge Street inclusive) were served by alternate trains.

It was not just the service that was altered: fares changed as well. Almost unheard of in the modern age, a series of fare reductions of up to 50% was announced in January 1910. Examples are: Hendon Central to Warren Street or Euston reduced from 4d to 3d, Hendon Central to Belsize Park, 3d to 2d, and Camden Town to Goodge Street, 1½d to 1d. Fares that halved were Golders Green to Belsize Park, 2d to 1d, and Hampstead to Camden Town, 2d to 1d. In-town journeys, between Goodge Street and Charing Cross, all remained at 1d.

It seems likely that the reductions were to drive an increase in traffic on the line. Many of the reductions were to Hampstead, Golders Green, and Hendon, where this would encourage further growth of the new suburbs. Other fares might have been reduced to compete with specific bus services.

In 1906 proposals had been made for the amalgamation of the three Yerkes tubes into one single company. Although a Bill was prepared for the 1907 session of Parliament it was never deposited. The American shareholders were the problem, feeling that there was a greater potential financial return if the tubes remained separate.

The situation was rather different three years later. The original traffic forecasts had been seen to be greatly over-optimistic, and the UERL had been narrowly rescued from financial crisis. The efficiencies of a single company now countered any residual transatlantic concerns. The result was the London Electric Railway Act of 1910, under which the GNP&BR absorbed the Bakerloo and Hampstead tubes, and was renamed the London Electric Railway Company (LER). This amalgamation had been approved at the share-holders' meetings of all three companies, held on 17th February 1910 at the Westminster Palace Hotel.

Workmen's fares were also revised: single tickets were scrapped, but returns could now be purchased until 08.00 covering journeys across the LER. The advantages that this gave outweighed the abolition of single tickets, and the Bill was therefore strongly supported by the LCC, which usually strenuously opposed any reduction in their availability.

The London Electric Railway came into being on 1st July 1910. Its first Chairman was Lord George Hamilton, and the Managing Director was Albert Stanley, promoted from his role as General Manager of the UERL. By 1912 negotiations were in progress between the various underground railway companies concerning further amalgamation. Competition with the various bus companies had intensified, especially with the development of viable motor buses. The LER was in a powerful position, with its tube railways extending out of the central area, to help grow the traffic. The same could not be said for the CLR, whose traffic was falling due to competition from motor buses; the C&SLR, whose traffic was static; and the GN&CR, which had traffic growth, but which overall was still very low. The Metropolitan Railway (MR) was still a force to be reckoned with, and it too was involved in the negotiations.

The outcome was that the MR acquired the GN&CR, which it intended to connect with its own line near Liverpool Street, and use for goods traffic. The LER purchased both remaining tube railways. This was seen as a threat by the MR, which drew up Heads of Agreement with the LER concerning the C&SLR. This forbade the connection of the Bakerloo with the C&SLR by extension of either, as this would threaten their traffic on the Inner Circle. The LER and MDR were not to oppose the extension of the GN&CR, and the MDR was to grant the MR running powers between Hammersmith and Richmond.

An early poster for Hampstead Heath by Nancy Smith.

THE FIRST EXTENSION

One of the annoyances for the commuting public was the lack of interchange at Charing Cross between the various Underground railways. The Metropolitan District Railway had a station on the Victoria Embankment, at the southern end of the main-line station, called Charing Cross; this had direct passenger interchange with the Bakerloo, although the latter station was called Embankment. At the northern end of the main-line station lay the terminus of the Hampstead Tube, also called Charing Cross. However, passengers wanting to get to the MDR had to exit to the surface, walk down Villiers Street, and enter the MDR station. The Bakerloo line was reached via a long sloping passageway descending from the level of the District Railway, and this too was seen as an inconvenience.

The first plans to bridge this gap were discussed in early 1909, and by May the UERL's engineer James Chapman had placed details before the Board. After being asked to calculate the costs of construction, Chapman found that the arches of the Hungerford railway bridge were on piled foundations that would conflict with his planned route. On 12th October he submitted revised plans, and the Board decided to proceed with a Bill for the extension in the 1910 session of Parliament.

The Bill sought powers to construct an extension south-eastwards of just over 800 feet between the Hampstead and District stations. Rather than having a standard two-platform terminus in which trains would reverse, it was decided to construct a loop with a single platform, allowing trains to run through more efficiently. With up to 44 trains per hour running on the line south of Camden Town, this solution would bring distinct advantages. The southbound tunnel would be extended eastwards under the Victoria Embankment Gardens to a point just north of the MDR station buildings, where it would start to curve round to the south, continuing under the river as it did so. It would pass beneath the bridge carrying the SE&CR from Charing Cross station before crossing back under the Embankment near the junction with Northumberland Avenue. Finally it would pass under Craven Street and the main-line station before joining up with the existing northbound tunnel.

Two trailing sidings would also have been constructed. These would have allowed defective trains to be stabled until it was convenient to return them to Golders Green depot. One would have been built under Victoria Embankment Gardens, and the other south-east from the southernmost point of the loop — under the Thames! All construction would be performed from staging in the river as well, to minimize disruption to nearby streets and buildings. The only land required was an LCC storage yard under Charing Cross Bridge between the Embankment and Embankment Place; this would become a new entrance to the station.

Facing page The Strand entrance to Charing Cross station in about 1909–10. This was located at the western side of the station forecourt, and consisted of a staircase descending to the sub-surface ticket hall. Note the inconsistency in the line names: Hampstead & Highgate Rly on the large sign, yet Hampstead Tube shown at the stairwell. This was not unusual in the early days.

The siting of the single platform became a problem for the railway company. In order to make interchange as convenient as possible it needed to be adjacent to the Bakerloo platforms, on the south side of the loop. This meant that the large station tunnel would be very close to the foundations of the Hotel Metropole, who raised considerable opposition. Had the ground been good for tunnelling, the company might have been successful, but unfortunately it was not. In order to achieve a satisfactory gradient the loop had to be above the level of the Bakerloo tunnels, which were crossed either side of their platforms. The lower 7 feet of the new tunnel would be in clay, but the upper section was waterlogged sand and gravel. The owners of the hotel brought a succession of engineers before the House of Lords Committee that was considering the scheme, all of whom highlighted the considerable risk of subsidence. Dalrymple-Hay could not muster sufficient support, and the Lords decided that the loop should not proceed as planned.

Undeterred, the LER modified their plan to meet the objections and resubmitted it the following year. The London Electric Railway Act of 2nd June 1911 authorized the extension, in the form of a single-track loop 880 yards long. The existing southbound tunnel would be prolonged southwards, parallel to Villiers Street but curving eastwards to pass under the Victoria Embankment Gardens. The direction of curvature would then reverse, with the loop being formed under the Embankment and extending 65 yards under the Thames, before continuing inland again to run parallel with the main-line railway bridge under Villiers Street. It would then connect to the northbound tunnel of the existing railway. The whole station could be reconstructed at the same time, including the installation of escalators, to make interchange between all of the lines easier. This was quite a radical step, as there were no escalators yet in service on the Underground railways, although a pair was under construction at Earl's Court on the Piccadilly line, and opened on 4th October 1911.

The contractors, John Mowlem & Company, started work on the £100,000 project in October 1911. The problems were managed by making a large open excavation 65 feet deep and 66 feet long adjacent to the western edge of the substation. This latter structure was underpinned on brick arches, with the supports descending to the level of the base of the new Hampstead Tube platform tunnel. The tunnelling shield necessary for the construction of the rest of the loop tunnel was assembled from the base of another shaft sunk on the river side of the MDR, beneath the Charing Cross railway bridge. The tunnelling was performed in compressed air, to hold back the water in the soil. With only 18–36 inches of clay above the tunnel where it passed under the Thames it was essential to keep the pressure balanced with the tide, and a gauge was installed on the Charing Cross landing stage. Hourly readings were taken and used to adjust the air pressure.

The loop had a sharp curve of 231ft radius to minimize its distance from the Embankment, and the track subsequently installed was superelevated to ensure that trains could round the loop comfortably at 25mph. With the tunnel so close below the riverbed, concerns existed about dredging in the main river channel damaging the tunnel, and so it was kept as far from the channel as possible. It had a diameter of 12ft 9ins — larger than normal, to allow for the overhanging ends of tube cars as they rounded the curve. As it passed under the District line, the cast-iron tunnel was constructed within a larger brick tunnel to minimize the risk of damage to the older line. The construction under the river took from 2nd November 1912 until 6th March 1913 to complete.

50

The station was built as a single platform with noticeable curvature, even though it was located on one of the shallowest curves of the new loop (albeit a reverse curve). Two new escalators ascended from platform level to a new concourse constructed directly below the District tracks and platforms. Short staircases connected these with the concourse. To improve the links with the Bakerloo, a further pair of escalators descended from the concourse to a landing above the level of the Bakerloo platforms. A staircase descended the final 10 feet to the southbound platform, whilst a new subway and staircase bridged the two platform tunnels to allow access to the northbound. A long passageway on a gentle gradient was provided for those passengers who wanted to change between the Bakerloo and Hampstead tubes.

The escalators to the Bakerloo opened on 2nd March 1914, and were a great success, with the number of passengers interchanging up by around 25 per cent. Just over a month later, on 6th April the new loop and station on the Hampstead Tube opened, taking the name Charing Cross (Embankment); the original Charing Cross station on the Hampstead Tube became Charing Cross (Strand) on the same day. On the same day the Bakerloo station was similarly renamed, giving naming consistency to the stations for the first time since they had all been open.

The Hampstead Tube escalators were the eleventh and twelfth to come into service on the Underground and were of the Otis A type (identical to those at Earl's Court, so-called because they were the first type of commercial escalators manufactured). They contained a large number of wooden parts, including the steps and the balustrades. Both pairs installed at Embankment were of the 'shunt' design, where passengers had to step sideways to leave the machine. Each pair consisted of one ascending and one reversible machine, ensuring that an escalator would always be available for traffic towards street level. The escalators were all installed in their own individual shafts.

The original ventilation shaft at Charing Cross (Strand) had been removed as part of the works. In its place a new shaft was sunk near to the District line with three times the capacity (60,000ft^3/minute). A washing screen and ozone apparatus (very popular at the time on the Underground, as it supposedly freshened the air) was also included. The latter equipment had been trialled on the CLR from 1911, and more recently at Goodge Street. The Hampstead Tube platforms at Euston were also receiving 'ozonizing' plant.

At the end of 1914 the new station building at Charing Cross (Embankment) opened, its completion having been delayed by a building strike. Designed by Harry Ford, it was single-storey, constructed of white Portland stone, with a glazed skylight over the ticket hall. A black and white chequered floor was laid in the latter space. The building exterior remains roughly the same today, although many internal re-arrangements have taken place over the years.

Notwithstanding the larger tunnel size on the loop, trains encountered problems with the sharp curve, and metal plates had to be welded on to their ends to prevent damage. The other issue was that the loop turned trains around. Previously the trains had all faced the same way, making it easy to form the electrical and air pipe connections between them. If a turned train attempted to couple with one that was not turned, then the connections would need to cross over between the car ends, which was most undesirable as the gatemen stood in this position. Additional rolling stock was provided to provide some spare cars, and a labelling system introduced so that the orientation of cars and trains could be easily seen.

TOWARDS THE TWENTIES

Traffic on the railway had grown steadily, although it had not reached the wildly optimistic levels forecast in 1905 by the UERL. The railway followed a useful route, opening up access to the villages of Hampstead and Highgate, linking the main-line stations of Charing Cross and Euston, and providing a good north-south route across the centre of London. The development of Golders Green kept the passenger numbers rising, and the extension to Charing Cross improved the traffic levels by providing better interchange.

It was not just commuter traffic that the railway sought, although this brought in much of the railway's income. Weekend trips to Hampstead Heath were advertised as early as 1907. Another event that drew the crowds was located north-west of Golders Green. Hendon aerodrome, established by the aviator Claude Grahame-White in 1910, staged its first 'aerial derby' in 1912, attracting hundreds of thousands of spectators. Buses were laid on to carry the crowds from the station at Golders Green, where the queues were long, and many chose to walk between the station and the aerodrome rather than shuffle along waiting for a space on a bus. The flying displays continued until 1914, when they were interrupted by the onset of war.

In 1912 the LER was excitedly describing its plans for the extension of the Golders Green branch to Edgware. The original Edgware & Hampstead Railway powers were expiring, and so a new Bill had been prepared for the 1912 session of Parliament. This completed the takeover of the E&HR by the LER, and the purchase of land for the extension continued in earnest. By the following year much of the route had been acquired and fenced in.

In late 1913 it was decided to promote a spur to connect the extension to the Midland Railway near to where they would cross at Hendon. However, the LER Bill for 1914 contained a lot of new works, and by November 1913 it was decided to drop the Hendon connection from the Bill for lack of preparation time.

In 1913 the Underground Group had acquired the Central London and the City & South London Railways. The latter is of particular relevance here, as plans were quickly drawn up for connecting it with the Hampstead Tube at Camden Town. In fact these were submitted to Parliament before the purchase was completed, and were authorized in the LER Act of 1913. A new section of tunnel would be constructed between Euston (where both lines had stations at different levels) and Camden Town. Other changes were made at Euston station in 1914. Much of the passenger traffic for the two tube railways was interchanging with the main-line station; in consequence the two tube ticket halls were lightly used, and from 30th September 1914 both closed

Facing page A 1912 poster for Hampstead Heath, designed for the railway by Walter Spradbery.

53

for an experimental period. The following May this was deemed to be a success, with no complaints received from passengers, and so the closure was made permanent. The station building was put to good use the following year when the adjacent substation was extended into it. This was linked with works to supply the C&SLR from the main Underground power station at Lots Road.

The First World War inevitably delayed the extension plans for the tube railways, although the extension of the Bakerloo Railway to Queen's Park that was under way when war broke out was completed in 1915. The authorized extension to Edgware was under a time limit (as were all railway Bills); however, given the unusual circumstances the powers were kept alive by the BoT under the Special Acts (Extension of Time) Act 1915, which was part of the emergency war legislation. This was used every year from 1915 until 1922, after which time the powers were extended through the conventional process.

The war years brought about many changes on the Underground. The passenger numbers rose steadily, helped in part by the reduced number of buses on the streets (over 1,000 were despatched to France for troop transportation). By the end of the war over half of London's local passenger traffic was travelling by Underground.

Of course, there was also an impact on employment. Over 3,000 staff enlisted during the course of the conflict, which led to women being employed in roles that had traditionally been barred to them, such as ticket collecting, operating the gates on trains, and maintenance work.

When Zeppelins began dropping bombs on the capital at the end of May 1915, it was not surprising that many people took shelter in the stations. This was accepted by the railway company and the Government, with the latter reimbursing the former for the extra costs involved with staffing and lighting the stations throughout the nights. Although it might be expected that this would be a recipe for trouble, the situation was handled well by both the shelterers and the authorities, and minimal inconvenience was caused to the regular passengers.

In 1917 main-line railway fares were increased by 50 per cent across the country. This was not copied by the London Electric Railway, which unlike the other railways was not under Government control. The LER felt that any such rise would be unreasonable given their profitable rise in passenger numbers. However, as the year went on it was decided that some sort of rise was necessary, and so it was announced that as from 1st September fares would increase. The company did take pains to point out that in most cases the increase would be low compared with inflation, and the average rise was less than 25 per cent. Their rise should have been higher, as over the war years costs doubled, but when they increased fares again in 1919 the company was heavily criticized by Parliament and the public.

The main problem facing the tubes towards the end of the war was overcrowding. The number of passengers had risen by 67 per cent since 1914, but very few new trains had been built. The problem was worsened by the large number of London buses that had not returned from war service in France.

The extension of the Hampstead Tube and the rebuilding of Charing Cross station in 1914 had proved a great success. So much so that congestion was being caused by the 130,000 people using the station each day. Passenger flows conflicted at the lower concourse level, below the District Railway, and so an extra subway was required. This proved to be a challenge, as it had to squeeze beneath the railway, and was below the water table. The chosen solution involved constructing the foundation as a cast-

A booking clerk with the Automaticket machine installed at Leicester Square station in 1921.

iron tank to keep the water out, and to use extensive insulation around the ceiling to minimize noise from the trains running 18 inches overhead. The 60ft length of passage cost £12,000, and opened to the public on 6th December 1920.

Congestion of a different sort occurred at Leicester Square station. The ticket office found itself struggling to cope with the theatre traffic, which effectively caused a second evening rush hour, and so a temporary booking office was installed in 1921. This opened between 16.00 and midnight, and was equipped with an 'Automaticket' machine, which sold tickets at 2d, 3d, 4d, 5d, and 6d values. The machine also allowed the booking clerk to issue up to five tickets of the same denomination with the push of a button, thus speeding up transactions for groups. It was estimated that 40 passengers per minute could be served. The success of these machines led to them being installed at new stations on the Hendon extension (described in the next chapter) from the outset.

At the request of restaurant managers in the West End of London, additional late night trains were run from Leicester Square to Highgate and Golders Green in 1921. They departed shortly before 01.00, but did not prove to be a success. Just 24 passengers used the two trains when a count was performed on 24th November.

The theatre express trains, having been withdrawn during the war, were reintroduced between 1922 and 1924. They ran non-stop from Tottenham Court Road to Golders Green, leaving Charing Cross after 23.00 (the times varied), calling at Strand, Leicester Square and Tottenham Court Road, and then running non-stop to either Hampstead or Highgate.

55

THE EDGWARE EXTENSION

The early history of the Edgware & Hampstead Railway has been told previously. The financial problems of the early years of the CCE&HR had prevented work from starting, even though the rapid growth of Golders Green showed the potential of extending into the countryside to the north. It was only once the First World War was over that thoughts once again turned to extension plans, and in 1919 Frank Pick, the Commercial Manager for the UERL, prepared a report. Included in his report were proposals to extend the Highgate branch north to the London & North Eastern Railway's Highgate station, and on to Alexandra Palace and High Barnet. This seems to have been proposed without regard to the engineering constraints, as the gradients of any line linking the two Highgate stations would be prohibitive. For the Hampstead branch, the extension was proposed as far as Hendon, where it would connect with the Midland Railway and run over the main-line tracks as far as Harpenden.

Pick gave evidence to the Select Committee on Transport (Metropolitan Area), also in 1919. He described the Edgware & Hampstead Railway as 'perhaps the most urgent extension of the present tube system', and expected work to commence within a year. He noted that 40 trains per hour were operated during the peaks on the Hampstead line; the absolute maximum with the current equipment was 43. After the connection to the C&SLR the company would work to raise this to 50, though this was never achieved. The extension to Hendon would be a 'fast line' with just three stations in two miles. This would be a change from the original lines, which had closely spaced stations, and extra stations added after the lines were authorized (e.g., Mornington Crescent) to ensure that as many people as possible would use the new railway. It was soon found that this slowed the train service, and this was explained to passengers as being the reason for the introduction of non-stopping where practical. Extensions of the 1920s and 1930s spaced the stations more widely, relying on buses to act as feeders. Since the Underground Group's acquisition of bus operators from 1912, this policy made eminent sense.

In 1921 high unemployment caused the Government to encourage works that would help alleviate the situation. A Trade Facilities Act was passed that year, providing a guarantee for necessary capital and interest, and the UERL wasted no time in submitting a £6 million scheme that now proposed extending the Hampstead branch to Edgware. This complete scheme was rejected because of great opposition by the LCC, who objected to part of the plan that would prevent any new bus operators from being licensed in London for ten years. However, a slightly modified £5 million proposal, with the bus clauses removed, did find favour. The money was raised as 4½% debenture stock, with a 50–year Government guarantee.

Facing page Edgware station with tracks laid and roof in place. There still appears to be a lot to do to get it ready for passengers, yet this photograph was taken in August 1924, a week before opening.

One of the key difficulties for the Edgware extension was caused by the very success of the Hampstead Tube. West of the terminus at Golders Green the path had been quickly blocked by housing development, and as early as 1909 the company was forced to apply to Parliament for an Act that deviated the planned route of the E&HR around the expanding estates. Over a mile of the route immediately north of the station at Golders Green was deviated because of the encroachment of housing onto the original alignment. In fact, the railway was pushed to the south-west side of Golders Green Road to skirt around the new parades of shops and houses that were being erected. Although most of the land had been bought by 1913, it was a narrow route forced to twist between the houses and streets in its path to the north-west. A number of houses still needed to be bought up, and in some cases only one half of a semi-detached house was purchased to save money. The occupiers of the remaining half would be left very close to the new line. At Colindale a number of houses occupied by the working class were in the way of the line, and the railway very quickly met its obligations to rehouse them. Under the 'Housing of the Working Classes Act 1903' railways were obliged to report on, and rehouse, the occupiers of any working class houses that were to undergo compulsory purchase. The occupiers had to be rehoused in equivalent accommodation at the expense of the company. In this instance three houses were involved, and their families were moved across the street into similar houses.

A ridge of high ground north of Hendon formed another obstacle to the railway. The Midland Railway main-line into London skirted its west side. In 1902 the E&HR Act had proposed a tunnel through the ridge, descending steeply at 1 in 42 before emerging into a cutting that would be spanned by a bridge carrying the Midland Railway. The latter was not happy at the disruption that the construction work would entail; it would also be left with a series of bridges that would need maintaining (even if at the expense of the Hampstead Railway).

Eventually, to overcome these objections it was decided to extend the tunnel northwards through the Burroughs Ridge in a pair of tube tunnels 5 furlongs (1 km) long, slightly curved, and on a gradient of 1 in 67. Their maximum depth would be around 70 feet, and they would pass beneath the Midland Railway. This was approved in the E&HR Act of 1912, and moved the line slightly to the north. It connected at its eastern end with the deviation of 1909, leaving no traces of the original 1902 route east of the Midland Railway.

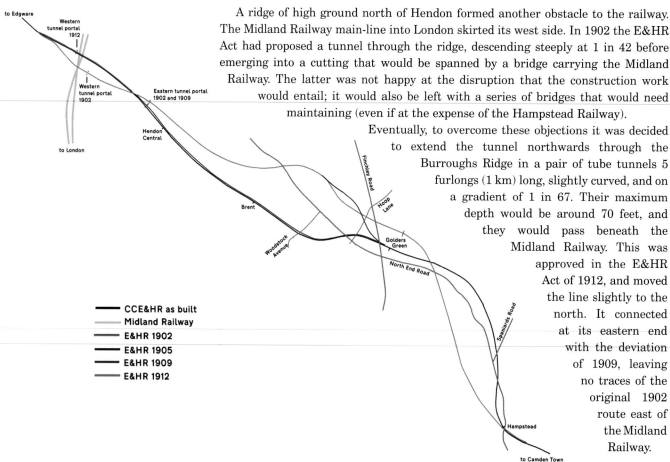

CCE&HR as built
Midland Railway
E&HR 1902
E&HR 1905
E&HR 1909
E&HR 1912

The other key items in the 1912 Act affected Golders Green and Brent, and involved replacing with viaduct a lot of embankment authorized in 1909. Viaducts were more expensive, but they took up a lot less land as they were only marginally wider than the railway. The rapid spread of houses meant that the railway company wanted to minimize the number of houses that required demolition. The original plan had been to cross the River Brent on embankment with just a single 56-yard length of viaduct. Now 151 yards of viaduct would be used. Likewise, between Highfield Avenue and Elmcroft Crescent 330 yards of viaduct would be built, with more further east between Woodstock Road and Finchley Road. A number of roads being laid out between Golders Green and Brent stations were acquired — this would prevent houses being built in the line of the tracks.

In December 1921 the *Railway Magazine* reported that the land for the extension had been purchased by the LER, and was ready for work to start immediately. The contract for the section between Golders Green and Hendon was awarded in 1922 to Charles Brand & Son, and work started on 12th June the same year. An official ceremony was held near to Highfield Avenue, with the President of the Board of Trade and MP for Hendon, Sir Philip Lloyd-Greame cutting the first sod and Underground Group Managing Director Lord Ashfield turning it over, both under the watchful eyes of invited journalists. Four months later the second contract, comprising the works between Hendon and Edgware, was awarded to the Foundation Company, for £258,468.

Progress on the line was rapid. By the end of the year the viaducts through Golders Green and across the River Brent were taking shape, and the station site at Hendon had been cleared. Some £38,000 was spent at Golders Green in adding a fifth platform face (by turning the eastern platform into an island, and converting a siding into the new southbound main running line). A new canopy was built for this platform on the back of the existing one, leaving the structure looking curiously unbalanced. A new staircase was also provided up to the central platform; the two sets of stairs pass with their landings at the same level in an unusual configuration.

The Managing Director of the Underground Group, Albert Stanley, had been knighted in 1914, and became Baron Ashfield of Southwell in 1920 in recognition of his work for the Government during the First World War. This official photograph shows him turning the first sod of the Edgware extension.

In 1923 the 250-ton girders for the bridge over Finchley Road were lifted into position.

Health and safety concerns were rather less in December 1922, when this photograph of Hoop Lane Bridge construction work was taken.

The track layout was also modified to handle the new services. It was explained to the press that the traffic levels at the station warranted this improvement, now being at around 12 million passengers per year. The outer tracks were signalled to allow trains to pass through without stopping, but (for signalling reasons) trains using the centre track would have to halt. New sidings were added to the depot, and a short dead-end tunnel was created on the north side of the existing tunnel mouths to enable the future 7-car trains to clear the newly repositioned points. Outside the station, plans were afoot to create a tram terminus alongside the bus station. This never materialized; between 1924 and 1929 Hendon Council was to thwart five such schemes.

A brick viaduct was constructed for the majority of the line between Golders Green and Brent stations. Once the section on the far side of the Finchley Road was completed a large steel girder bridge was put into place. Similar bridges were built across most of the other roads in the path of the line; that at Elmcroft Crescent was the largest on the extension, 129ft 6ins long and weighing 450 tons. At Woodstock Avenue the level of the road was raised by 7 feet to pass over the line, leaving a number of houses partially hidden by the road and with steps leading down to their doors and what remained of the front gardens. This was one of the locations where one-half of a semi-detached house remained adjacent to the line. One road further north, Montpellier Rise, was just severed by the line, and has remained in two halves ever since, again with severed semi-detached houses either side. The fall in the land level at this point made it impossible to raise the road level to pass over the line, and also too difficult to burrow the road under the line. The only bridge over a road not constructed from steel girders was at Hoop Lane, where an arch of Staffordshire blue bricks was constructed. The reason for this difference is unknown.

The viaduct and embankment at Brent were particularly wide, so that the island platform for the station could be accommodated here, as well as space for additional tracks to be constructed at a later date. Northwards the viaduct increased to a height of 34 feet to pass over the slight valley carved by the River Brent. Altogether some 8 million bricks were used to construct the viaducts, bridges, and other engineering structures on the section to Hendon.

Two small cuttings were also required. The first was on the southern side of Woodstock Avenue; without this, the road would have needed raising by an even larger amount. The second, a far larger cutting, started north of the Brent viaduct and continued all the way to Hendon station. Altogether over 80,000 cubic yards of soil was excavated for these, nearly half of which was reused to make embankments. Large steam excavators were used for the heavy earth moving.

The tunnels at Hendon, known variously as the Burroughs Tunnels or Hendon Tunnels, were constructed in an identical manner to the other tube tunnels in London. Tunnelling started at their north-western ends, with the first 400 feet being dug by hand using picks and shovels. This was the section beneath the Midland mainline, and in order to protect that railway further once the tunnel was dug, the lining was encased in 6 feet of concrete.

After this section was complete, rotary excavators were brought in to complete the tunnels. Continuous working enabled progress to be made at a rate of 60 feet per day, allowing the tunnels to be completed in nine months. Some 90,000 tons (of soil was removed from the site, and replaced with 6,400 tons of cast-iron lining. The standard tunnel telephone wires were installed throughout both tunnels.

North of the tunnel portals the line was far easier to construct, being almost at surface level for the whole distance except for a cutting at Colindale, which was constructed with concrete retaining walls, and a low embankment south of Burnt Oak. The entire formation was wide enough to accommodate an additional track should traffic demand in the future. Bridges at Colindale and Burnt Oak were constructed with sufficient width for such a track as well.

Six wagons of soil are removed from the cutting near Hendon by a contractor's steam locomotive. Behind, a steam shed continues to cut away at the earth.

The station at Colindale typifies the Georgian style of stations on the extension. It was badly damaged in the Second World War, and a temporary structure provided until its permanent replacement in 1962.

The station architecture was different to the previous designs employed on the tubes. Stanley Heaps, the in-house architect, designed each station in Georgian style, with white stone Doric columns supporting a projecting stone canopy at the front of each building. The station name was placed in metal letters along the front of this. The buildings behind were of brick construction with a steel frame, allowing for additional storeys to be added at a later date. A tiled, pitched roof was built above the ticket halls, which had clerestory windows below roof level to maximize the interior light. Beyond the wooden doors at the entrances, black-and-white chequerboard stone flooring was to be found. Free-standing oak Passimeter ticket offices were used, allowing one member of staff to issue and check tickets from the same location. The Board of Trade inspector was certainly impressed. In his report made just before the line to Hendon was opened, he wrote

This hall is remarkable for architectural features seldom to be found in English railway stations. The Company are to be congratulated upon the appearance, as well as the details of the building, from the point of view of facilities for passengers.

A similar style was used for all of the station interiors on the Edgware extension. This shows the booking hall at Brent with a wooden Passimeter.

Brent station with construction still in progress. The platforms are on an embankment, and space was provided to the side of the tracks to install passing loops.

All of the intermediate stations had island platforms 350 feet long with stairs leading either up or down to them. They were illuminated with incandescent lamps in pairs on poles, which had the station name roundels fitted either side. These were initially on temporary-looking square boards, but photographs show that they were replaced later in 1924 by large enamelled signs.

Edgware station, as befitted the terminus, was a larger building, Italianate in design with two wings extending forward and either side of a bus forecourt. Shops were provided in these wings. The main station building did not feature a separate stone canopy, but instead the pitched roof was brought forward along the length of the building. In the ticket hall, polished oak and bronze were used for the fittings. Like the other stations it had an island platform, but this was situated beneath a large glazed overall roof.

Burnt Oak station also differed from the general style. A small temporary brick building was provided, as initially the area was surrounded by farmland. It was not until 1928 that the 'proper' building, as designed by Heaps, was completed, although this was somewhat less imposing than the other stations on the extension, largely to keep costs down.

Edgware station was built to a larger plan, and included a forecourt for buses to turn around.

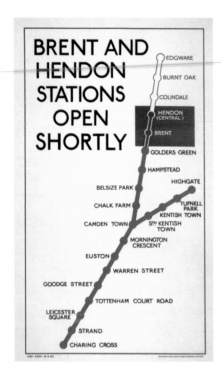

BRENT AND HENDON STATIONS OPEN SHORTLY

EDGWARE
BURNT OAK
COLINDALE
HENDON (CENTRAL)
BRENT
GOLDERS GREEN
HAMPSTEAD
HIGHGATE
BELSIZE PARK
CHALK FARM
TUFNELL PARK
KENTISH TOWN
CAMDEN TOWN
S™ KENTISH TOWN
MORNINGTON CRESCENT
EUSTON
WARREN STREET
GOODGE STREET
TOTTENHAM COURT ROAD
LEICESTER SQUARE
STRAND
CHARING CROSS

Prior to opening, and for some months afterwards, the new station at Hendon was known as Hendon (Central). The parentheses quietly disappeared from maps issued by the LER by about 1927.

A substation was also constructed at Burnt Oak. This was the first unstaffed substation on the system, a fact that generated much interest in the press. It was equipped with two 1,200 KW rotary converters (with space left for a third), which were remotely controlled from Golders Green substation. In order to supply sufficient electricity for the extension, another 15,000 KW turbo-generator was installed at Lots Road power station.

Another innovation for the extension was the use of colour-light signals throughout. Previously these had only been used in the tunnel sections of line, with traditional semaphore signals being used in the open. The new signals were clearer though, being visible from a distance of 2,000 feet. The points were electric, unlike the electro-pneumatic installations on the rest of the line. Signal boxes were provided at Brent (in anticipation of the installation of passing loops), and Hendon (to reverse the services initially). Colindale had a signal box to control the central reversing siding to the north of the platform, and Edgware, of course, needed a box to manage the terminating trains and access to a new depot constructed adjacent to the station. This depot had four roads, each with an inspection pit, in a long shed constructed in a similar style to the overall roof for the platform area. Four sidings were sited to the east of the car shed, giving the depot a total capacity of 76 cars.

The first stage of the extension was opened on 19th November 1923 with Sir Philip Lloyd-Greame returning less than 18 months after he had cut the first sod. At Golders Green he switched on the current to the new line, and was then carried with other dignitaries on the first train to Hendon. After inspecting the new station the party returned to Golders Green, where luncheon was held in the depot, in an echo of the original ceremony over 16 years previously. The King, the Government, and the LER and its extension were all toasted. In the speeches that followed, Lord Ashfield praised those staff and contractors involved in the construction of the extension.

The public was admitted to the new stations at Brent and Hendon (Central) from 15.00, and contemporary photographs show a large crowd waiting at the latter station with a policeman in attendance. The station buildings were decorated with flags and bunting. New trains were used and almost all were extended to run north to Hendon, with a train around every 3½ minutes, making the journey to Golders Green and London over 17 minutes shorter than before, when the buses provided the link between Hendon and Golders Green. Since Hendon was not the ultimate terminus for the extension, two crossovers were installed south of the station allowing trains to use both platforms. These were controlled by a signal cabin built at the north end of the station above a relay room. A similar cabin and relay room were provided at Brent.

On 18th August 1924 the section to Edgware was opened. As was usual for these occasions, the press were invited to inspect the new facilities, with lunch and entertainment laid on. A builders' strike delayed completion of Burnt Oak station, and this was not opened until 27th October. The same strike had delayed finishing some of the details at Colindale and Edgware, but this was not sufficient to prevent them from being opened. With the removal of Hendon Central as a terminus the signal cabin and one of the crossovers were redundant. The crossover was removed in 1926, but the cabin lasted another 11 years. The relay room was retained to house the destination indicator equipment.

Development along the recently built A41 is seen opposite Hendon Central station shortly after its opening.

Hendon Central station, with the entrances to the Burroughs tunnel beyond. The electrified tracks stop alongside the signal box, so the extension to Edgware is not yet open. The temporary platform signs show the name as Hendon (Central).

After construction work had started, tentative plans were drawn up for a new branch from the extension. A report dated January 1923 suggested a number of extension schemes for the LER that could be progressed for their 1924 Bill. The link to the Midland Railway at Hendon, mentioned in Frank Pick's report of 1919 was discussed again. It was felt that Harpenden was not far enough, and that the trains should be projected out as far as Luton. Intermediate stations would be at Mill Hill, Elstree, Radlett, Napsbury, St Albans, Chiltern Green, and Luton. Overall, a great deal of new line would be obtained with very little construction required.

The distances involved were cited as a possible problem. A new type of rolling stock would be needed (even though that on the Hampstead Line was just being replaced). It would need a top speed of around 45mph, allowing it to average 35 mph including station stops. Only with these speeds could people living 30 miles distant from London make the commute in 45 minutes. The trains would require more transverse seating, and unless the general standard of Underground rolling stock were improved, first-class accommodation would be needed. Space should also be considered for luggage and parcels. In short, a main-line train of tube dimensions was necessary. Ultimately none of the schemes listed in the report were developed for the 1924 LER Bill.

The railway initially seemed reluctant for some reason to use the name Burnt Oak for the station serving that neighbourhood. A sign was erected on site in summer 1923 stating that the new station would be named Sheaves Hill. Prompted by this sign, on 10th September 1923 Hendon Urban District Council wrote to the London Electric Railway suggesting that, if Burnt Oak was not considered a suitable name, Orange Hill or Deansbrook might be considered as alternatives, as Sheaves Hill 'would not convey to the minds of many people' where it was. In the end, the name Burnt Oak was decided on before the new station opened.

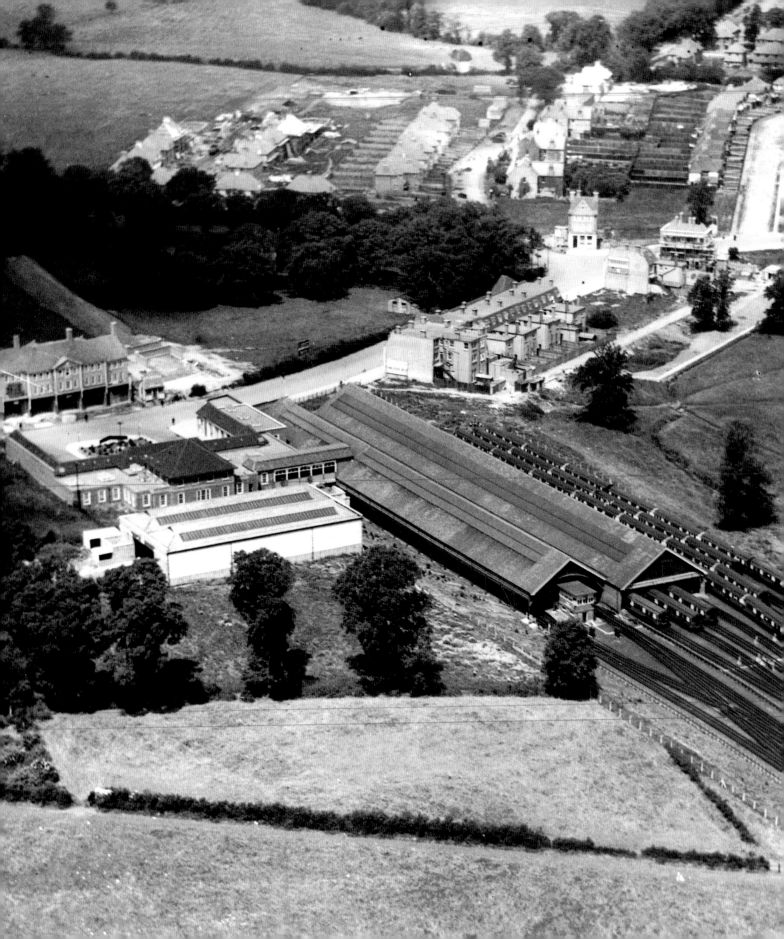

THE GROWTH OF THE SUBURBS

As with the original decision to extend the CCE&HR to Golders Green, the intention was to grow the suburbs northwards to create traffic for the extension. Aerial photographs of the area before the arrival of the railway show very little but undeveloped farmland.

Hendon was a well-established village when the extension opened. The Midland Railway had opened its station in 1868, and this had already caused the village to increase in size. A number of new streets with terraces of housing were laid out before the end of the 1800s. Ribbon development had occurred either side of the road linking the village with the main-line station, which was about a mile distant. However, the new Underground station was constructed in open land to the south-west of the village. A large roundabout was laid out in front of the station, which the company optimistically referred to as 'the Piccadilly Circus of North West London'. The land in this area had been raised by 14 feet by the railway in the course of its construction. Shops and offices were built around Central Circus, a number being sold before the end of 1923 and only just after construction had started.

Within five years of being opened as a free-standing building, the station had been incorporated into a large parade of shops. Three additional storeys containing flats were erected above, as originally intended, all linked with the buildings either side. The complex was given the imposing name of 'Central Mansions'.

Colindale station had a small number of houses nearby, courtesy of the airfield. Workers' houses had been constructed during the war, and some terraced cottages were built around a square called Aeroville to the north of the station site.

It was the purchase of 390 acres of land next to Burnt Oak station by the LCC that made the station viable. The land was used for the Watling estate, consisting of 4,021 houses and flats designed in a style similar to the garden suburbs. A light railway was laid from the LNER at Mill Hill (The Hale) to bring in building materials, and the LER constructed the section of Watling Avenue between the station and the main road to Edgware (the original intention was for it to be called Mill Hill Avenue). The growth in population on the estate was dramatic: from just over 1,000 in 1921 to 19,012 by 1937. Private housing was constructed to the north and west of the estate, further stimulated by the construction of good quality bypass roads in 1927 (Watford Way and Edgware Way).

At Edgware another enterprising estate agent called George Cross bought up 70 acres of land from late 1919 in anticipation of the railway. Part of the land was purchased by the LER for the station; the rest was sold off as building plots. Sales were initially slow, and in 1924 Cross paid for some houses to be built to help drive

Cover of a booklet giving details of places to live along the line of the new tube.

Facing page Edgware station in 1926. The parade of shops opposite the station is nearing completion, and houses are being built nearby. The route beyond Edgware is also visible, with the parapets of a bridge constructed behind the shops.

Below New housing spreads out to the north of Brent station shown here on 4th March 1926.

Facing page top Houses under construction in Rundell Crescent, Hendon, looking towards Vivian Avenue.

Facing page bottom Bank and shops with flats above nearing completion at the junction of Vivian Avenue and the A41, opposite Hendon Central station.

up demand, which sold for £1,100 each. He also developed a parade of shops to the north of the station. Another developer erected a row of shops across the road from the station; this incorporated a concrete raft below Nos. 30 and 31 to allow the railway to be extended towards Watford beneath the buildings without disturbing them.

As at Golders Green land prices along the route had soared, and there was good money to be made. Initial signs were good, with the railway reporting to its staff in December 1923 that

> Already at Hendon (Central), shops and residences are springing up… during the last 12 months, 687 houses, etc., have been erected, and plans have been passed for a further 1,500 houses. The local authorities have prepared plans for construction of 15 miles of new roadway.

However, the extension did not prove to be the immediate success that the LER had predicted. Unlike the situation at Golders Green in the early 1900s, the speculators seemed content with buying and selling land for profit, and housing development was of secondary interest. In early 1927 Lord Ashfield addressed the shareholders at a meeting and noted that traffic had risen from 594,000 in December 1925 to 674,000 in December 1926, a 14 per cent rise. This was disappointingly low, and he placed the blame on the land speculation.

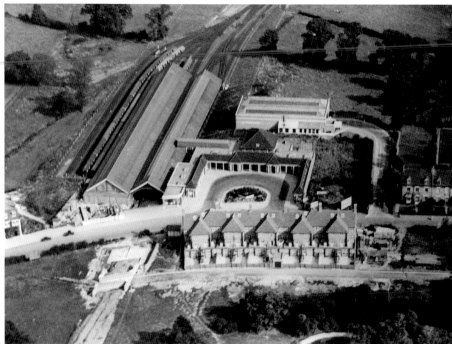

The rural nature of Edgware at the time of the Hampstead Tube's arrival is shown in a contemporary poster and an aerial photo from 1926, which also shows the provision made for extension of the line beyond Edgware.

An extensive advertising campaign was in place, exhorting people to move from London out to the fresh air of Edgware. As the fields disappeared beneath bricks and mortar, the advertisement images changed to show attractive country houses, and emphasized the low cost of commuting, especially with a season ticket. The LER kept fares artificially low on the extension (by comparison with the nearby main-line railways) to help drive the growth of traffic. Without a trace of irony the LER had written in the opening brochure for the Hendon extension:

> As a final note the Underground Company wish to state that they have done all in their power to preserve the rural aspect of the new districts which have now been penetrated. The rough earth embankments are turning into grassy slopes, and the bridges (upon which no advertisements will be placed) have been made as sightly as possible consistent with stability. A scheme is now in hand for planting trees and shrubs along the line.

This was the extent of rurality for the line, as in the Edgware extension brochure the company pointed out that 'the fields traversed by the Underground between Colindale and Edgware are admirably adapted to housing schemes of every kind'. It seemed that grassy embankments and lineside shrubs would be the only greenery left in the vicinity of the new railway.

Traffic rose 45 per cent in 1927, largely attributable to the Watling estate starting to be populated. This in turn had repercussions: those living closer in to London could no longer get a seat, or even board the trains. More trains from Golders Green were promised, as were longer trains. It was not until 1929, when the service was increased to 29 trains per hour, that the passing loops were installed at Brent station on the wide viaduct. They were signalled for trains to run through at 40–45 mph.

One event that always boosted traffic was the Hendon air show. The airfield at Hendon had been requisitioned by the RAF in 1914 for the duration of the war. They returned in 1920 for a pageant, and two years later took over the site completely. The pageants included spectacular flying displays that drew huge crowds like those of 1912–14. Many of the spectators travelled by tube to Colindale, instead of taking the bus from Golders Green as they had before the war. These pageants continued right up to the Second World War, with those of 1938 and 1939 being termed 'Empire Air Days'. The only mishap to significantly affect the Underground occurred on 5th August 1935, when an aircraft having mechanical problems crashed on the tracks near Colindale. The pilot was killed, and the short circuit caused a fire to ignite in the signal cabin, which was destroyed. Services planned to reverse at Colindale were not operated for several days, presumably being extended to Edgware or cancelled.

In 1922 Frank Pick, in his role as Joint Assistant Managing Director of the Underground Group, had purchased the Watford & Edgware Railway, which by that time had no remaining powers but still remained a legal entity. The following year a report was produced by the Group in which the completion of this railway was listed as an objective. It was considered that the route would include the traffic centres of Stanmore, Bushey Heath, and Bushey, before terminating at the large town of Watford.

In late 1924 the Watford extension came very close to being included in the next LER Bill. Planning for the route had been done, but there were difficulties in securing some necessary land in Edgware at a reasonable price. The scheme fell into abeyance, but was not totally forgotten. A bridge was constructed over the course of the line just behind the shopping parade in Edgware, and land purchases continued along the route. The story of the line beyond Edgware continues on page 104.

The photograph (left below) was taken on 28th June 1930, and shows the enormous crowds returning to Colindale station after a Royal Pageant at RAF Hendon.

A driving motor car constructed by the Metropolitan Carriage, Wagon & Finance Company in 1923.

In order to provide a frequent service along the extensions new trains were required. The existing rolling stock was almost 20 years old, and combined with the need for new trains on the City & South London Railway (see next chapter), it was decided to go for a completely new fleet of trains. Following experiments that started in 1911 and culminated in a small batch of stock ordered in 1919, it had been recognized that the gate ends of the existing cars were inconvenient to the public, and placing pneumatically operated sliding doors in the centre of each car side was preferable. If passengers could be loaded and unloaded faster, then the train service could be increased, and the number of train staff could be reduced to three (from five, for a 5-car train).

Five manufacturers were invited to construct sample trailer cars to a similar specification. On four of these the interior styling was left to the manufacturers, but the fifth was designed by Underground staff. They were demonstrated to the press on the Piccadilly Tube in early 1923 and formed into a train with gate stock motor cars at each end. They were then transferred to the Hampstead Tube and entered service in August 1923.

In March 1923 an order was placed for 191 new cars based on the Underground's design of prototype. The order was split between Cammell Laird, the Metropolitan Carriage Wagon & Finance Company (MCW&FC), and the Birmingham Railway Carriage & Wagon Company. For legal and financial purposes the C&SLR owned 69 of the cars, with the rest belonging to the London Electric Railway. Deliveries started in late 1923, with the cars being sent straight to the Hampstead Tube at Golders Green depot. As the combined pair of tube lines grew, more cars were needed, with another 127 ordered in May 1924 in anticipation of the extension of the C&SLR south to Morden (31 of these would be owned by the C&SLR). A further 120 were ordered in 1925 for the extension of the Hampstead Tube to Kennington (described in the next chapter), and also to lengthen the existing trains to seven cars. Fourteen of these were vested in the C&SLR.

The trailers and control trailers were the first tube cars to feature two pairs of

An interior view of one of the 1923 trailer cars, this one constructed by Cammell Laird.

double sliding doors on each side; the motor cars had one pair of sliding doors with a central pillar between them. A swing door was fitted at the guard's position, at the rear of each motor car. For safety reasons these doors were locked out of use when a guard was not present. This was tested by the same electrical circuit that proved all of the passenger doors to be closed – without this proof the guard was not able to send the starting signal to the driver. A large equipment compartment was situated behind the driver's cab, housing the electro-pneumatic control equipment for the train.

This compartment somewhat reduced the seating capacity in these cars, to just 30 people. The trailers and control trailers seated 48 and 44 respectively. For the benefit of those passengers bereft of a seat, vertical handrails were fitted at the door vestibules, and grab handles along the clerestory ceiling. Incandescent lamps were used with frosted glass shades.

The exteriors were painted red below the windows with cream up to the roofline, and a grey-painted roof. Black bands separated the colours. The doors and ends of each car were painted solid red up to the roof. Inside, the dark woodwork was combined with paintwork in cream and 'cerulean blue' (which is actually green).

Upon the opening of the Hendon and Edgware extensions, the new stock was introduced onto the Hampstead Tube. The original gate stock was still in use, and initially the two stocks were used for all journeys. However, it was soon found that the brakes of the older stock worked less well in the open, and the services were adjusted to keep it operating in the tunnels as far as possible. One other feature of interest is that two guards were carried until around 1927. The guard at the rear of the train checked that the doors were all closed; he signalled to the other guard at the front of the train (sometimes called the 'front conductor'). This latter individual would give the starting signal to the driver. Once the air-operated doors had proved to work well in service (and the initial teething problems had been overcome), it was decided to eliminate the front conductor. A telephone between the rear guard and the driver first had to be fitted to all of the trains to allow them to communicate.

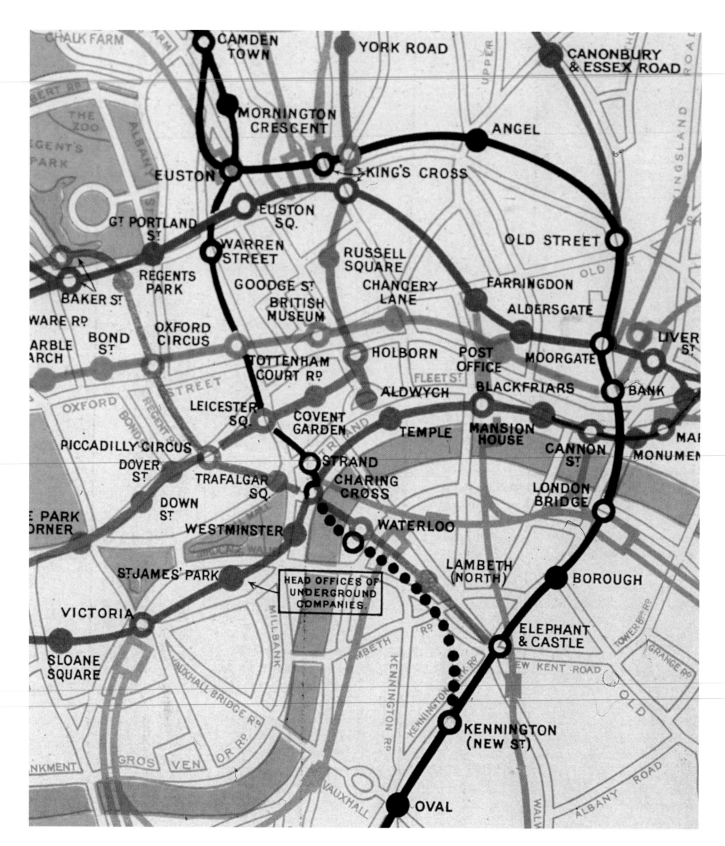

LINKING TO THE C&SLR

As far back as 1913, when the C&SLR had been purchased by the UERL, the possibility of connecting it with the Hampstead Tube to make better use of both lines had been mooted. The Hampstead line terminated in central London at Charing Cross, giving an unbalanced effect, suggestive that it could conveniently be extended southwards. The C&SLR likewise finished awkwardly at Euston in the north, and Clapham in the south.

The solution was to create a short length of tunnel to link the two railways at Euston, thus balancing the two northern branches with two routes across central London, and this was duly authorized in the LER Act of 1913. A problem was posed by the restricted running tunnels of the C&SLR, and so the C&SLR Act of the same year gave authority for the reconstruction of its tunnels to LER standards. The possibility of just enlarging the smallest sections of tunnel was toyed with for a while, thus leaving the whole line with a minimum diameter of 10ft 6ins. The engineers went as far as designing a smaller version of the standard tube rolling stock to prove that it was feasible. This idea would have meant it remaining incompatible with the other tubes, and the small trains would have been required on the Hampstead Tube when connected to the C&SLR, restricting its capacity. Fortunately, full-size reconstruction was eventually undertaken.

The First World War prevented the works from starting, as the energies of the LER were directed towards completing the Bakerloo extension to Queen's Park. Once things started to return to normal it was found that rising costs necessitated additional funding, and so another two Acts for the LER and C&SLR were passed in 1919 permitting the companies to raise a further £2.5 million.

The £6 million scheme proposed by the UERL in the light of the passing of the Trade Facilities Act in 1921 (mentioned in the previous chapter) included the C&SLR modernization and the Euston connection. Another scheme was also put forward in a report of June 1922 for the extension of the Hampstead Tube southwards from Charing Cross to meet the C&SLR at Kennington. Authorized by the LER Act of 1923, this was part of a scheme to fully integrate the two railways and extend the C&SLR deep into south London, an area that hitherto had been very poorly served by the Underground. This was partly because of the geology south of the Thames; rather than the heavy clays, which were excellent for tunnelling but found mostly north of the river, south London is dominated by water-bearing gravels. The other reason was the fierce opposition raised by the main-line railway companies to any planned extension of the tubes into what they considered to be their territory.

One minor change occurred on the maps: from the early 1920s the Hampstead Tube began to appear in red. This was a short-lived change, as it soon became black (or dark grey) to match the C&SLR once the planned connections were shown in 1924. Around the same time the key on the maps began to term it the 'Hampstead and Highgate Line'.

Although both railways had stations at Euston they were positioned such that it was not possible to effect a junction in the immediate vicinity of the station. Since the intention was to allow C&SLR trains access to the northern branches of the Hampstead Tube it was necessary to swing the new tunnels of the former around in a northward curve and join them south of the existing bifurcation at Camden Town, an extension some 5,000 feet long. In order to achieve this some sharp curves of 420ft radius were required, constructed in 12ft 6ins diameter tunnels to allow for the overhang on the cars. The gradients were also steep in places. Although it was an extension of the C&SLR, the work was carried out by the LER.

Work started on the connection from the C&SLR to the Hampstead Tube in August 1922 when the contractors, Mowlem, sank three shafts. Two of these were at Mornington Crescent, and the other was at Ampthill Square, immediately to the west of the Hampstead Road and north of the LNWR main-lines. The latter shaft was for the construction of the pair of running tunnels between Euston station and the new junctions at Camden. Short lengths of the tunnels at this point were constructed using compressed air, because of a pocket of waterlogged sand in the clay.

The shafts at Mornington Crescent permitted the construction of the most complicated junction ever built on the Underground network, and were located in the road junction north of the station, and positioned so that they passed between the two platforms. One was 80ft deep, with an 8ft diameter access heading leading off to access the southbound works, and the other was 60ft deep, with a similar heading to access the northbound works. The difference in depth resulted from the need when the original line was constructed to place the northbound and southbound junctions at different levels so that there would be no conflicting train movements. The works took place beneath Mornington Crescent station, which has its platforms at a depth of just under 49 feet.

Chambers, in which the Greathead tunnelling shields were erected, were mined out, each being 15ft in diameter. Tunnelling proceeded both northward and southward from each chamber, allowing the delicate work of constructing the new junctions to continue apace. Trains continued to run on the Hampstead Tube, and hence any works requiring access to existing tunnels had to take place in the short period each night when services ceased.

The new northbound tunnel for trains heading to Golders Green was brought into use shortly after construction was completed, in order to assist with the rest of the tunnelling. By diverting northbound trains away from the original route, the complex business of connecting the northbound route from the C&SLR could be made easier. In the southbound direction a new more easterly tunnel from Highgate was opened first. Both of these works moved the junction between the two northern branches further south, and were dug by hand at the north end where they intersected the original tunnels. The space between the new junction and the site of the old was then used to intricately link the tunnels to the C&SLR at Euston. The result is that south of Camden Town there are now six parallel running tunnels for a distance of around half a mile.

The works involved the construction of four new step-plate junction tunnels (cone-shaped chambers allowing two tubes to merge into one), and two skewed cylindrical junctions, each 25ft in diameter. The skewed cylinders were constructed by adapting the original step-plate junctions. Seventeen connections were made between the old and new tunnels, and the operation of the CCE&HR trains was not impeded in any way. The company was proud to announce that the greatest error in alignment between the tunnels was only a quarter of an inch.

The signal cabin at the south end of the northbound Highgate branch platform was re-equipped to handle the increased complexity of the junction. A 43-lever Westinghouse frame (of which six levers were spare) was installed, described by the *Railway Magazine* as 'the largest of its type in the British Isles'. Alongside was a new illuminated track diagram showing the position of the trains in the vicinity. The junction was signalled to a capacity of 40 trains per hour from each branch, or a total of 160 trains per hour in both directions. The signal cabin at Mornington Crescent was taken out of use at the same time, and control of the crossover transferred to the Camden Town cabin.

Tunnellers working in a Greathead shield near Mornington Crescent in December 1922. The soil removed to make the new tunnels weighed 80,000 tons, and around 13,000 tons of tunnel lining was installed in its place. Much of the work was done by hand, especially at Camden Town with the existing tunnels nearby.

The connection between the Hampstead Tube and the City & South London Railway at Camden Town opened on 20th April 1924 and this poster shows the tunnelling layout that achieved it. The junctions here permit trains travelling from both southern branches to reach either northern branch without conflicting (and vice-versa).

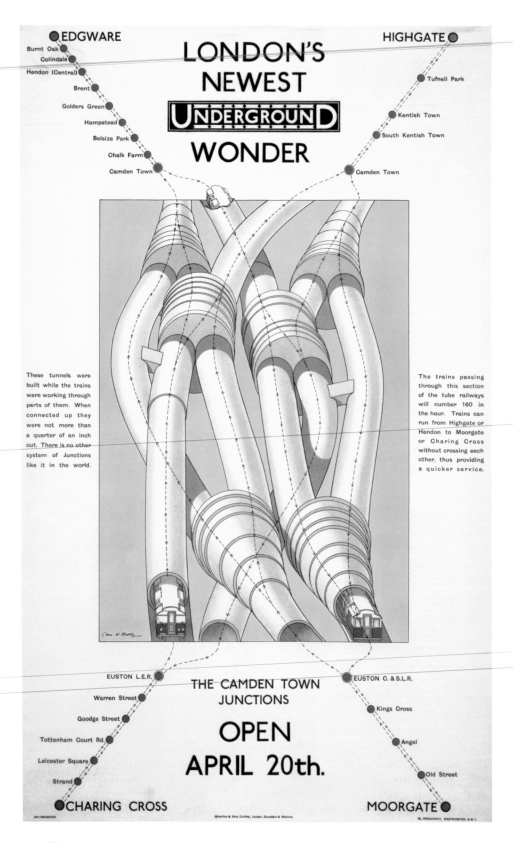

The link between the two tube railways opened for service on 20th April 1924. Reconstruction work on the C&SLR was not yet complete, and trains were only running between Euston and Moorgate (which was called Moorgate Street prior to closure). Anthony Bull, who was 15 at the time and whose father was a friend of Lord Ashfield, drove the first train on the line from Highgate to Moorgate. It started just after 08.00, and took 20 minutes. This young man, who was to become Vice Chairman of London Transport between 1965 and 1969, was presented with an engraved driver's reverser key. The line was then opened to the public, with a 7-minute service operating to each of the northern termini from Moorgate, giving a 3½-minute service between Camden Town and Moorgate. The following month the company proudly reported that the Camden Town Junctions were now handling 1,504 trains per day as against 1,080 prior to their reconstruction. This service comprised:

- Charing Cross – Golders Green: 251 trains per day each way
- Charing Cross – Highgate: 250 trains per day each way
- Moorgate – Hendon: 126 trains per day each way
- Moorgate – Highgate: 125 trains per day each way

During the rush hours 96 trains per hour passed through, which equated to a train every 37 seconds. The LER confidently reported that this was not the limit of what could be achieved.

When the C&SLR did reopen between Clapham Common and Moorgate on 1st December 1924 a service of 26 trains per hour was run, dividing equally at Camden Town. The new rolling stock described in the previous chapter was also introduced, and for the opening ceremony Lord Ashfield's daughter Marian drove one of these trains to Clapham Common. An original train of C&SLR rolling stock was stabled in the adjacent platform to allow comparisons to be made between the old and new. At the same time the C&SLR was renamed 'The City Railway'.

The extension of the Hampstead Tube southwards to join the C&SLR at Kennington was an idea of the 1920s. In a report from 1922 it was noted that it would reduce congestion on the Bakerloo line, with an estimated 8.9 million passengers using it in preference. A single intermediate station would be constructed at Waterloo, thus providing additional access to the West End from the main-line station. At Kennington additional platforms would be provided, and a loop south of the station would replace that to be lost at Charing Cross. The C&SLR south of Kennington would be extended from its terminus at Clapham Common to Morden, where it would connect to the Wimbledon & Sutton Railway. The latter was authorized in 1910, but had remained dormant and in the ownership of the UERL.

A final part of the scheme proposed to form a series of junctions with the Bakerloo Tube, allowing trains from Clapham (and as far as Sutton) to operate to Watford over that line. Four short sections of tunnel would form connections beneath Waterloo station and Westminster Bridge Road, allowing trains to pass between the Bakerloo and Hampstead tubes. The steepest connection would be at 1 in 55.

Once constructed, trains would be able to run from either southern terminus of Elephant & Castle or Clapham Common (and Sutton, once the C&SLR was extended), to any of the northern termini of Watford Junction, Golders Green (and eventually Edgware), and Highgate. It is debatable as to whether such complexity would have helped or hindered the service, bearing in mind the disruption that the Northern line suffers today with its many junctions.

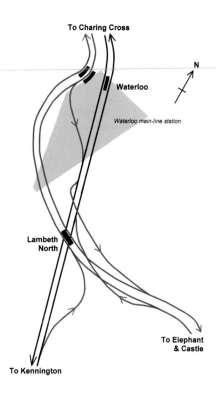

To Charing Cross

N

Waterloo

Waterloo main-line station

Lambeth
North

To Elephant
& Castle

To Kennington

A plan showing the proposed
connections between the Bakerloo and
Hampstead lines.

The plans as described were deposited with Parliament for the 1923 session. They were initially rejected by the House of Lords because of the opposition of the newly formed Southern Railway (SR), which operated the main-line services south of the Thames. Negotiations were rapidly held between the UERL and the main-line company and the plans were revised in time for the next meeting of the Lords Committee that was examining the Bill.

The amended railway plan made no attempt to go south of Morden. Unfortunately the SR objected to the Bakerloo junction tunnel beneath Waterloo station, which linked the southbound Bakerloo to the southbound Hampstead, and would allow Bakerloo trains south to Clapham. The main-line railway was planning an underground line of their own beneath Waterloo, with main-line trains descending into the tunnel at Nine Elms and running round a loop before returning to the south-west. An underground platform on the loop would connect via escalators with the main-line station above. The junctions between the Bakerloo and Hampstead lines were, to some extent, an all-or-nothing scheme, and reluctantly the LER accepted that what has been described in *Rails Through the Clay* as "south London's 'Camden Town'" was not to be.

Another protest had been raised by the owners of the Old Vic theatre, who discovered that the plans were for a shaft to be sunk right outside their property. Naturally the ire of actors and theatregoers was incurred, and a petition was deposited against the Bill. The LER recognized the negative publicity that this was causing, and on 17th July reached an agreement with the theatre. The shaft would not be dug at this point, and the petition would be withdrawn.

Royal Assent was given on 2nd August 1923. In October a prospectus was issued for a new issue of 4½% debenture stock, totalling £2,356,000 for the LER and £3,769,000 for the C&SLR. The purpose of this extra capital was to fund the Kennington and Morden extensions, as well as the reconstruction of Piccadilly Circus and Leicester Square stations.

Work started on the extension to Morden on 31st December 1923, on the site of the new Clapham South station. It was not until April 1924 it was noted in the press that two barges were moored near Hungerford Bridge from which borings were being made to determine the condition of the soil along the route of the new line between Charing Cross and Kennington. On 22nd April construction work started.

The majority of the tunnelling was carried out from sites south of the river. At Waterloo a first shield chamber was formed on the site of the northbound platform, and then, via a cross-heading, a second was formed on the southbound alignment. The running tunnels northwards under the river were then started. Two shafts were dug in the grounds of Bethlem Hospital (which became the Imperial War Museum in November 1935). From their lower level four shields were used, two working north to Waterloo and the others south to Kennington. The southbound tunnel at Kennington encountered a layer of rock 2ft thick in the clay, which had to be broken out by hand as the tunnel progressed. This tunnel passed beneath the C&SLR, with a clearance of just 2ft 6ins to the southbound tunnel of the latter railway.

A new platform was also required at Charing Cross, as the extension of 1914 had provided just a single platform on the loop. Fortunately this original platform was in such a position as to be usable as the new northbound platform. The new southbound platform was constructed 230ft south of where the new line diverged from the loop under Villiers Street. A shaft was sunk at the south end of Buckingham Street, in the

Victoria Embankment Gardens, and from here access was made to the site of the platform. A shield was erected in a large chamber and worked southwards for 350 feet to form the station tunnel. To the north the running tunnel was dug by hand.

The final construction site was on the northern edge of Kennington Park. Here the southernmost point of the loop passed under the C&SLR tunnels. A shaft sunk in the park provided access, and a 400ft length was constructed in compressed air due to a layer of wet sand. The rest of the loop was constructed in the normal clay.

At 08.35 on 19th January 1925 an unusual accident occurred on the Charing Cross loop when two trains collided. A defective train was being sent round the loop so it could return to the depot at Golders Green. Two trains were stuck in the loop behind, whilst successive trains were being reversed at Strand. One of these trains, being of the new rolling stock and longer than the old gate stock, was forced to trip past a red signal at the south end of Strand in order to clear the crossover tracks so it could reverse; it was first emptied of passengers. After this had happened the signalman then decided to allow it to proceed south around the loop, as the defective train was moving again. The driver was authorized to proceed with caution. Owing to a misunderstanding the driver went further than intended, and with the very limited visibility in the tightly curved loop ran into the rear of the next train. The driver of the rear train had his leg badly crushed and broken, the guard of the front train was injured, and a passenger and two gatemen received minor injuries. Some damage was caused to both trains. The passengers in the two trains on the loop were led onto the tracks and into the platform at Charing Cross on foot.

By October 1925 *The Times* was able to report that around three-quarters of the tunnels were complete, including the southbound platform tunnel at Waterloo. The northbound running tunnel was under the bed of the Thames, and the southbound not far behind. The Greathead tunnelling shields heading southwards were, it was estimated, three months away from Kennington. The contract for the crossovers and a new reversing siding there was awarded at the same time, and all tunnelling for the extension was expected to be complete by spring 1926.

It was never going to be possible to cut through the Charing Cross loop without disrupting the train service, and from 25th January 1926 the services were restricted. All trains from Highgate terminated in the southbound platform at the original Strand terminus, and reversed south-to-north over the crossover north of the station. Trains originating from Edgware used the crossover to reach the northbound line at Strand, on which they ran southbound to the platform at Charing Cross. With a few exceptions these trains did not stop for passengers at Strand. The few passengers wanting to make the short journey between the two stations were advised to take the first train to Leicester Square and return southbound on the correct train. The Traffic Notice describing these points generously noted that passengers would not be charged extra for travelling one stop beyond Strand by mistake.

To ensure that the service was reversed as quickly as possible, a second driver boarded the rear cab at Strand. As soon as the passengers had changed at Charing Cross he could then drive the train northwards. Meanwhile, the original driver would make his way through the train to the north end, and disembark at Strand (via the motorman's cab door) ready for the next train. By March 1926 it was noted that '98 cars per hour' were operating to Charing Cross in the peaks — which equates to fourteen 7-car trains, giving each just over 4¼ minutes to get from Strand, unload, load, and return to Strand.

In the loop tunnel the lining was dismantled at the point where the new south-bound running tunnel would cut through. Rough brickwork was used to fill the tunnel in this section, whilst concrete was used to fill a length of about 12ft either side. South of the existing platform at Charing Cross a temporary brick wall was constructed to seal off the tunnelling works from the public areas of the station. More rough brickwork was used in the tunnel to the south, where the new tunnel would connect, and concrete again filled the section round to the new southbound line. The tunnelling shields from Waterloo proceeded northwards, with the brick sections being dismantled when they were reached. The new northbound tunnel then connected into the end of the new platform tunnel built some time earlier.

Closer to the surface more station reconstruction was started in January 1926 in order to cope with the congestion that still plagued Charing Cross station. It was the busiest station on the Underground system, handling 35 million passengers a year by 1928. A larger concourse beneath the tracks of the District Railway was excavated, and escalator shafts were mined to the new southbound platform. These were fitted with Otis L-type escalators, and opened to the public on 15th November 1926 and 18th July 1927. The first escalators on the Underground at shallow level (i.e., not being placed into specially dug shafts) were opened on 10th December 1928, linking the concourse with the ticket hall. This was extended to three times its original size, some 13,000 square ft (1,209 m²), and provided with Passimeters and 20 new ticket machines. It was proudly claimed that the reconstructed station could handle 50 million passengers each year, and was already served by 2,744 trains per day.

With the complex network of platforms and passageways present at Charing Cross, some experiments were made in passenger information. A floor sign was installed, consisting of glass letters reading 'To Edgware and Highgate Railway'. Lights beneath the blocks made the sign prominent to the passengers. Coloured lights were also used to indicate routes around the station: passengers would note the colour associated with their platform and follow a series of lamps situated in the passages – for example, blue for Waterloo trains.

Kennington station was also subjected to a major rearrangement. It was decided that cross-platform interchange between the pairs of platforms in each direction was desirable; however, both platforms were on the east side of the platform tunnels. The situation was resolved by widening the existing northbound running tunnel at each end of the station and switching the position of the track and the platform. Now the Hampstead line platforms could flank those of the City & South London Railway and provide the cross-platform interchange. The platform access also needed rearrangement as a consequence, and stairs were put in between each pair of platforms leading to a pair of passageways at a higher level. Instead of forcing passengers to use another set of stairs to reach the lower lift landing, the landing was moved 11 feet further up the shaft. The emergency staircase was similarly shortened, and the lower portion destroyed to make way for the new southbound platform.

The other works at Kennington were problematic as well. The reversing siding provided between the C&SLR lines south of the station, allowing trains from either branch of the new line to reverse south-to-north, was particularly difficult. There was a 10ft difference in height between the running lines, a legacy of the original station layout. The connection from the southbound tunnel led to a steep climb to the level of the northbound line before the actual siding was entered. Pockets of wet sand were encountered in the clay, making conditions treacherous for the miners, and the running tunnels either side had trains passing every 2–3 minutes. Nonetheless, the problems were overcome. By comparison, the station at Waterloo was more straight-forward. From the outset it was provided with a bank of three Otis L-type escalators. Some delicate underpinning of the main-line station was required; this structure is constructed on a huge brick viaduct, and it was essential that the pillars remained properly supported throughout the works. The shaft was through water-bearing ground, and so concrete walls were constructed around the area through which the shaft would pass, down to the level of the underlying clay. The waterlogged soil was then removed from within, and the box so created was filled with weak concrete through which the shaft was cut. The first escalator entered service on 29th July 1927, with the other two joining it on 12th and 13th October of the same year. Unusually the layout of the station meant that the central escalator was for descending passengers, with the outer two for ascending passengers arriving from the two tube lines. The lifts at the station remained in use because of the volume of passengers passing through.

A new substation was constructed adjacent to Lambeth North station on the Bakerloo line to supply power to the new section of railway. At this point the Hampstead Tube extension passes underneath the southern end of the Bakerloo station, and so a connection was easy to make. The substation was controlled remotely from Charing Cross substation, and contained two 1,500 KW rotary converters.

It was noted in the press that not only were many thousands of men employed in London for the works, the benefits that the extensions brought spread wider still. Middlesbrough and Nottingham benefited from the order of 2,000 tons of steel rails and 90,000 tons of cast-iron tunnel segments, and the 2,900 tons of bolts used to assemble these segments were made in Wolverhampton. Kent and Essex supplied the cement, with tiling and other ceramics coming from Staffordshire and Leeds. The electrical cables, signalling equipment, signage, and track fittings all derived from other major British industrial centres. Many of the tools used, such as pneumatic shovels, were also British-made; this had been driven by the demands of the Underground, as previously they had only been made overseas.

In order to help passengers find the right train on this most complex of Underground lines, destination indicators were installed on the platforms at Leicester Square, Tottenham Court Road, Charing Cross, Kennington, Euston, Bank, Moorgate, Waterloo, and Morden in July 1926. These illuminated the destinations for the next three trains and were probably the first of their type on the Underground.

The new link from Charing Cross to Kennington opened on Monday 13th September 1926 in conjunction with the extension of the City Railway southwards to Morden. A special train of the new rolling stock left Golders Green at 11.30, passed through the new station at Waterloo, and arrived at Clapham South station at 12.05. Here it waited for ten minutes whilst the guests inspected the surface parts of the station. The Parliamentary Secretary to the Minister for Transport, Lt-Colonel John Moore-Brabazon, MC, MP then took the controls of the train for the run to Morden. Here the train passed through to the new depot south of the station where a luncheon was laid on for the guests. As at the opening of the Hampstead Tube in 1907, speeches were made by the guests and officials of the railway company, with congratulations for the successful completion of this phase of Underground extensions. The public was admitted to the extension from 15.00. The local residents were provided with 15,000 free tickets, allowing them a return journey to Bank or Leicester Square.

The report of January 1923 outlining options for the 1924 LER Bill (mentioned in the previous chapter) also included plans for an extension of the Hampstead Tube southwards from Charing Cross, running via Brixton and Clapham Park to Streatham. The idea was that this would follow on from the Morden extension and Charing Cross to Kennington link. The extension could be built in two parts: the first from Kennington to Brixton, Clapham Park, and Lower Streatham; the second via stations at Norbury, Thornton Heath, North Croydon, South Croydon, to terminate at Sanderstead. The latter section would most likely have been on the surface, and used existing tracks, although no details were given. The benefits to the tube section would accrue from people transferring from road transport (which was described as being very heavy between Brixton and Streatham). At Kennington it would be a fairly easy matter to extend the line from the reversing loop, and then follow Brixton Road and Brixton Hill southwards. As with the other schemes in the report this scheme was not developed any further.

The 1920s were a decade of labour unrest, with the most serious events on the Underground railways occurring in 1924 and 1926. The events of 1924 started in late March, with the trades unions deciding to call a strike of their members on the tubes in support of the striking tramway workers. Although the busmen who worked for the London General Omnibus Company (part of the UERL) walked out in sympathy, the railwaymen never actually took part.

It was at the beginning of June that the Underground was really affected. An unofficial strike was called, without the support of the unions, by what *The Times* called 'Communist agitators' seeking a significant increase in wages and other working conditions on the LER and Great Western Railway. The railway companies refused to negotiate with an unrecognized body, and at midnight on 4th June the strike began. It consisted mainly of unskilled and semi-skilled workers from the power stations and the workshops; the latter was less of an issue, but without electricity the railway could not run.

The effect was immediate and dramatic. The output of the Lots Road power station was cut by 60 per cent, and the train services dropped to half. Chaotic scenes ensued on the platforms as passengers struggled to find places on overcrowded trains. The effect on the Hampstead line was the closure of the stations at Strand, Goodge Street, Warren Street, Mornington Crescent, Chalk Farm, and the entirety of the Highgate branch. The NUR was most unhappy, seeing its authority being undermined as its members took unofficial action. The Electrical Trades Union (ETU) issued a statement noting that none of its members would strike, and that it was purely an issue for the NUR.

An 8-minute service operated between Charing Cross and Golders Green, with another shuttle service running from Golders Green to Hendon. The service did not degrade further on the line during the strike, although further station closures occurred elsewhere on the tubes. Conditions across the lines were overcrowded, with *The Times* noting that 'girl workers from shops and offices had to risk damage to hats and join in the crush for seats or standing room'. Passengers and the press rapidly lost any shred of sympathy they might have had for the strikers, who realized that they were in an impossible position because the railway companies refused to recognize them or their strike. The Government joined in, promising the fullest possible protection for those men willing to continue at work in defiance of their striking colleagues.

By Monday 9th June the situation had changed little. The unions were pressing the strike committee to call off the action, and met Lord Ashfield to inform him that they were working to improve the railway services. Services began to run between Camden Town and Highgate once more, although no intermediate stations were open; these services ran exclusively to Moorgate every 8 minutes. The following day Kentish Town reopened, but the service widened to every 10 minutes.

Just as people felt that the strike was on the verge of collapsing, the ETU announced that it was considering calling an official strike of its members at the power station. Fortunately this did not materialize, and on Friday 13th June the strikers returned to work. Power was rapidly restored, and by the end of the day all stations except for Mornington Crescent and South Kentish Town had reopened. These two stations, which had low passenger numbers, were kept closed as an experiment to speed up the traffic. Mornington Crescent reopened on 2nd July, but South Kentish Town was to remain forever closed.

The General Strike of 1926 started at midnight on 3rd/4th May, when the Trades Union Congress called all of its members out on strike in support of the miners. The result was the complete shut-down of the Underground as motormen, lift men, power station workers, and other staff withdrew their labour. An immediate call was put out for volunteers and this proved hugely successful. The Hampstead Tube reopened between Golders Green and Strand at around noon on 6th May, with volunteer train staff, and naval ratings running the power station at Lots Road. The service operated for the rest of the strike was around every 8 minutes, but not all of the stations were open. It was on 8th May that the Highgate branch reopened (but with all intermediate stations closed), and two days later a 15-minute shuttle service between Golders Green and Edgware resumed, calling at Hendon Central. By 11th May it was reported that the only sections of line devoid of service were the Hampstead between Strand and Charing Cross, and the Piccadilly's short branch from Holborn to Aldwych. Hampstead, Chalk Farm, Euston, Warren Street, Goodge Street, and Charing Cross stations all remained closed until around 12th May, the last day of the strike.

The General Strike was not the first occasion when volunteers were used to drive Underground trains. On 26th September 1919 a national railway strike began under the auspices of the National Union of Railwaymen (NUR), the cause being a dispute over wages and conditions. During the war, pay for railwaymen had been increased via a War Bonus. After the war the companies decided to standardize wages, but in such a way that some grades would see their pay cut. Although the pay settlement did not affect the Underground staff, workers at the Lots Road power station joined the strikers in sympathy. This immediately caused a massive reduction in the number of trains run, but the effect was short-lived as by 29th September the power station was operational again using volunteer labour. Volunteers were also sought to drive the trains, and practised on the District and Hampstead Railways to provide them with some experience. Foremen and other technicians not on strike acted as instructors. The volunteers were put up in railway accommodation for the duration of the strike. The first day of training was on the operation of the trains. The next one-and-a-half days were spent being trained on a particular line, and the final afternoon covered the resolution of train faults. If the volunteers were judged to be competent after this intensive three-day course then they were passed out for driving on their own.

STATION AND OTHER IMPROVEMENTS

The huge growth in traffic since the opening of the tube lines was leading to severe congestion at some of the central London stations. New stations were provided with escalators, but at the original stations passengers were still obliged to wait for a lift to take them to the platform. Although some lifts were switched between stations to relieve particularly acute problems, only a radical change would bring long-term relief. In short, many stations needed expensive rebuilding to accommodate escalators.

The first of these major works was at Oxford Circus, when escalators to the Bakerloo line were introduced in 1914. The first Hampstead Tube station to benefit was Tottenham Court Road, where congestion was particularly acute. The LER Act of 1914 had granted powers to enlarge the station and link the Central London and Hampstead sections more effectively, but the war had once again delayed matters. In 1920 staff called 'hustlers' were introduced on the platforms to ensure that trains stopped for no longer than scheduled. A siren was sounded when the train was due to depart, with the intention that this would deter people from trying to board.

The 1914 powers were finally used in 1923 when work started on the construction of a new ticket hall beneath the St Giles Circus road junction. Two years later, on 28th September 1925, the ticket hall was opened, and with it a bank of three Otis L-type escalators descending to the level of the Central London Railway. Only one escalator was in use at this time, for ascending traffic in the morning and descending traffic in the evening, and some of the lifts remained in operation. The lower landing of these escalators passed through one of the old CLR lift shafts, still visible today and known as the 'rotunda'. Another pair of escalators was opened at the same time between the CLR level and the Hampstead Tube. The completion of the other escalators, and other works in the station continued. On 3rd February 1926 the outstanding pair of escalators was switched on and the remaining lifts at the station were withdrawn from service.

Permission had been sought at the time of the first escalators opening for their speed to be increased by 20 per cent from the standard of 90 ft/minute. Experiments were made with the CLR escalators at Bank station in October, and the Ministry of Transport (MoT) approved an increase of 11 per cent to 100 ft/min.

Camden Town station, although not in the heart of London, was in need of improvements, and on 7th October 1929 a pair of L-type escalators was opened between the ticket hall and the northbound platform level, with stairs to connect

Facing page The rebuilt entrance to Highgate station (now Archway), designed by the architect Charles Holden, was opened in 1931. This photograph was taken soon afterwards.

A view up the new escalator shaft being dug at Archway in December 1930.

to the southbound platforms. These low-level passages were new as well, with the original passageways at the southern end of the platforms being retained to provide additional capacity for people changing between the various services. Since the escalators were provided in a shaft with no other stairs, the emergency spiral stairs dating back to 1907 remained in use.

A new type of escalator from Otis, called the MH, was installed at Highgate station and opened to the public on 15th June 1931. Faster than the L-type, these were made in the USA and shipped to the UK; Otis built all subsequent MH escalators in Britain. The original spiral stairs remained in use for emergency purposes. A new octagonal ticket hall was provided at the same time, and Charles Holden, the architect responsible for the Morden extension stations, designed the façade of the new building in white render, resembling Portland stone.

In 1928 the lifts at Warren Street were equipped to operate automatically, saving on the cost of lift staff. This equipment was subsequently transferred to Earl's Court in 1932. This was probably connected with the reconstruction of Warren Street with two flights of escalators linking the ticket hall and platforms (each flight containing a pair of Otis MH-type escalators with stairs between). Work started in late 1930, and the escalators came into use on 27th September 1933. The station building was also rebuilt in the Portland stone style slightly further east, so that it opened onto Tottenham Court Road. The new ticket hall was opened in late 1934. Three storeys of flats were built over the station at a later date.

On the Highgate branch, Kentish Town also had a pair of MH escalators installed. These came into operation on 21st November 1932, together with a new ticket hall. Again, the original spiral staircase was retained.

The new building at Warren Street, faced with Portland stone, was fully opened in 1934.

The largest station reconstruction on the Hampstead line was at Leicester Square. It was necessary because by the late 1920s over 27 million people were using the station annually, and as noted in a previous chapter, the theatre traffic was particularly heavy. An increase in the speed of the lifts in 1925 and 1926 to 290 feet per minute, which was 45 per cent faster, saving 11 seconds per journey, had gone some way to improve matters, but nowhere near far enough. Work started in October 1930 and took almost five years to complete, with Mowlem and John Cochrane & Sons as contractors. A circular sub-surface ticket hall was constructed beneath the junction of Charing Cross Road and Cranbourn Street, and the existing station buildings were adapted to provide stairwells. This had the added advantage of allowing much of the building space to be rented out for commercial use.

Charing Cross Road had been constructed in 1887 by the LCC. In common with the other new roads provided by the Council, it had both a sewer and a pipe subway beneath. The latter was designed to accommodate the gas and water pipes, as well as any future utilities. Maintenance could be performed without the need to dig up the street. Unfortunately both the sewer and subway lay in the way of the new ticket hall. The first part of the station works therefore involved the construction of new tunnels for both, at a lower level and to the west of the station. A new pipe subway was provided below Cranbourn Street as part of the works; this passed beneath the Charing Cross Road pipe subway, but the two were connected as well. The sewer under Cranbourn Street was also diverted to the south to avoid the line of the escalators to the Piccadilly line. Other headings were also driven to assist with the rebuilding, and during the four years that the workmen were on site some grew mushrooms in the subterranean passages.

A shaft was then sunk under the station building, and horizontal headings made from this. The walls of the escalator machine rooms were constructed from these headings. The nearby buildings were underpinned, and then more headings just below the road surface were dug. In these were installed the girders to form the new ticket hall roof. These techniques allowed the road closures to be kept to a minimum.

The next task, whilst the ticket hall works continued, was to sink the escalator shafts. A separate bank of escalators was provided to each of the two tube lines to keep the passenger flows as separate as possible. The shafts were initially made 8ft in diameter, then enlarged to 14ft, and finally enlarged again to 22ft 9ins. Three MH escalators were installed in each shaft, those to the Hampstead line having a rise of 58ft 9½ins, and those to the Piccadilly line rising 80ft 9½ins. This latter trio were the longest escalators in the world at the time, being 161ft 6ins long. Pedestal uplighters were installed on the escalator balustrades to illuminate the shafts. The ticket hall and passageways were tiled with biscuit-coloured tiles, and included an attractive red and blue frieze based on the LT initials. The platforms were also retiled at this time.

The new ticket hall came into use on 4th May 1935, although one escalator had been used on 27th April to help manage the passengers attending the Cup Final that day. The press were taken around the station on 2nd May by J. P. Thomas, the General Manager of the London Passenger Transport Board (LPTB), and other officials. They noted the similarities with Piccadilly Circus, and also that two of the entrances were out of use as the lifts obstructed them. The lifts were to be removed as soon as the new ticket hall opened. One of the entrances on the west side of Charing Cross Road gave direct access into the Hippodrome.

A diagram of the new sub-surface ticket hall at Leicester Square was published in the *Railway Magazine*. Part of this concourse was badly damaged by an IRA bomb in 1939 (see page 111). The entrance from the corner of Charing Cross Road and Little Newport Street was permanently closed from around 1986, when a new ticket office was constructed in the area.

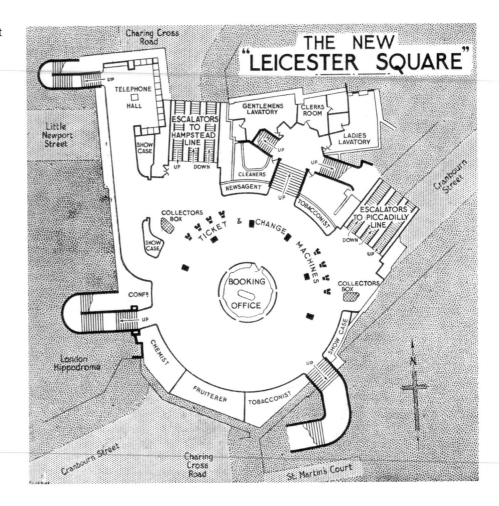

On 8th June 1936 the final two entrances were opened. These were part of a new Portland stone building on the corner of Charing Cross Road and Cranbourn Street, and a smaller corner site at Charing Cross Road and Little Newport Street.

The staff magazine for February 1924 reported that the lighting levels had been doubled on the platforms at Piccadilly Circus, Oxford Circus, Tottenham Court Road, Leicester Square and Charing Cross as an experiment. Tests carried out at the stations showed that the improved lighting sped up the passenger movement and 'encourages a livelier step'.

In late 1926 a third exit was provided at Golders Green, for passengers leaving northbound trains only. Situated half-way between the main building and Finchley Road it was designed to allow a faster interchange between the trains and trams, saving, it was estimated, three to four minutes. The northbound platform and stopping position for trains were extended northwards by about 50 feet. Although this exit has long closed, it can still be seen from the footpath along the front of the station. At the same time the main station ticket hall, unchanged since opening, was reconstructed. It was handling 40 times as many passengers as in 1907. A new single-storey structure with a pitched roof was added to the front of the existing building, taking it to the edge of the bus station. It was made of white-painted concrete and was surmounted by a large solid 'bullseye' name sign: it was not particularly attractive.

The decision was made to demolish the existing ticket offices inside the station and replace them with Passimeters, similar to the new stations on the extension northwards.

As well as the passenger stations, works were carried out on the electrical sub-stations for the tubes. In December 1930 a new substation was opened at Hendon Central. This served two purposes: firstly, to increase the power available on the Edgware branch, with its increasing train service; and secondly, as an experiment with a new piece of equipment. This was the mercury-vapour steel-tank rectifier, a device with no moving parts, and thus much quieter and lighter than the rotary converters used previously by the tube railways. The experiment was needed because six new substations would be opening in the early 1930s in connection with the Piccadilly line extension to Cockfosters. The success of the Hendon installation gave the Underground Group the confidence to specify rectifiers for the new substations. Rectifiers were also provided at another new substation at Leicester Square, constructed in Upper St Martin's Lane at the same time as the station was rebuilt.

As the traffic on the line increased, the company looked for ways to make the service more efficient. The introduction of non-stop trains was an early way to achieve this; the closure of South Kentish Town and Mornington Crescent (the latter temporarily) in 1924 was another. Mornington Crescent had its service altered again on 1st December 1924, from when all trains to and from Edgware non-stopped. The following year all the Edgware trains were routed to and from Charing Cross on weekdays; the Sunday service was changed similarly from 19th June 1927.

Edgware had an express service as well, departing at 08.58 and running non-stop to Golders Green. Mornington Crescent and Warren Street would then be skipped on the way into central London. This service used the passing loops at Brent station to overtake the previous train. A similar northbound service ran in the evenings, departing Tooting Broadway station at 17.12.

Earlier trains were put on for workmen from 24th September 1928, with the first leaving Edgware at 05.25. At the other extreme of the day the last train from Leicester Square departed at 00.34 as from November 1930. These times were adjusted again in 1931, but the essential features remained: a train every 2–3 minutes in the peak hours, every 5 minutes off-peak, and every 5–7 minutes on Sundays.

The end of the 1920s saw increasing pressure to co-ordinate the management of transport across London. This had been discussed many times since the early 1900s but nothing substantial had ever really resulted. The election of a Labour Government in 1929 changed all this though. The Minister of Transport, Herbert Morrison, was determined to see London's transport co-ordinated under public ownership. Through the parliamentary session of 1931 a Bill to this end was debated and approved, but another change of government caused delays, and it was not until 13th April 1933 that it received Royal Assent.

On 1st July 1933 the London Passenger Transport Board took over. It absorbed all of the Underground companies, as well as the Metropolitan Railway (much against the wishes of the management), the London General Omnibus Company (which was already part of the Underground Group), all independent bus companies in London and several tramway companies. To the public it quickly became established as London Transport. Its first Chairman was Lord Ashfield, with Frank Pick as Vice-Chairman.

The unattractive 1926 addition to the front of Golders Green station.

Myerscough — Walker / 39

92

A NEW NAME AND NEW WORKS

No line on the Underground has borne as many names as today's Northern line. The CCE&HR opened as the Hampstead Tube, or Hampstead Railway. By 1911 the concept of 'lines' had been adopted, with the Underground map for that year referring to the London Electric Railway's Bakerloo, Piccadilly, and Hampstead lines. Another official map from 1919 referred to it as the 'Highgate & Hampstead line'. This seemed to be used interchangeably with 'Hampstead & Highgate line' in the early 1920s, although the latter eventually won out, having been introduced when the connections with the C&SLR were under way. This name stuck for nearly a decade, at least on the maps issued by the company, with City & South London being retained for the other portion of the line. However, 'Hampstead & City line' was used for the pair of lines in some quarters.

Immediately after the opening of the extension to Morden, correspondents to *The Times* made some ugly suggestions based on the Bakerloo concept (a contraction of Baker Street & Waterloo), such as Edgmor, Mordedge, Edgmorden, and Morware; some added 'railway' into their contractions to form Medway and Medgeway, and one person suggested Moleway. Probably the simplest of all was the Eden Tube. Other suggestions were less ugly, such as the Surrey Tube, and the Morden Tube (which was already being used in the press). None were officially adopted though. 'Edgware, Highgate & Morden line' had been used on maps since the introduction of Harry Beck's new diagram in January 1933, until being shortened to the Morden-Edgware line from 16th June 1934.

Opposite A 1939 drawing of the new station being built at East Finchley for the arrival of the tube.

Signage at Euston station for the Morden–Edgware line, a name that lasted just three years.

With more extensions being planned it was realized that termini were an unsatis-factory way to name the line, especially one with multiple branches and routes, and the search started for a new name. The LPTB drew up a shortlist of nine.

After deliberation by a group headed up by J. P. Thomas, the name Northern line was chosen in February 1937, and was officially introduced on 28th August 1937. This name is used henceforth to avoid confusion.

A minute from the LPTB chairman's meeting of 11th February 1937 at which it was decided, somewhat reluctantly, to adopt the name 'Northern line'.

NAMES OF LINES : RAILWAYS   1031.

With reference to Minute No.982, Mr. J.P. Thomas reported that
he had circulated to twenty-three Principal Officers nine of the
most likely of the names which were considered in respect of the
Morden-Edgware group of lines, and that the result showing the
order of preference was as set out hereunder :-

        1. North South
        2. North and South
        3. Norsouth
        4. Northern
        5. Cross Town
        6. City
        7. Greater London
        8. Interborough
        9. City West

It was considered that none of the first three alternatives was
suitable and it was

        DECIDED: that in default of securing a better name for
                 the Morden-Edgware group of lines, the name
                 "Northern" be selected, subject to confirmation
                 by the Chairman.

Congestion on the Edgware branch became steadily worse as the 1920s drew to a close. In 1929 some 17 million passengers were using it, and the levels of discontent were rising. The branch was a victim of its own success – the rapid growth in housing, especially at Burnt Oak, was filling the trains almost from the start. More 7-car trains were promised (by adding an extra car to the 6-car trains that still formed around half the trains on the line). However, it was difficult to add extra trains without taking some away from other places, such as the Highgate branch. As it was, there were about 30 trains an hour via Charing Cross (and also via Bank) – one every 2 minutes. It was (and still is) difficult to run many more trains than this with heavy passenger traffic because of the time taken to unload and load at each station. Also, the more frequent the service the easier it is for a slight problem to escalate rapidly into a major delay. Most trains to and from the Edgware branch via Charing Cross passed through Mornington Crescent without stopping, which saved a minute or two. Changes were made to other non-stopping trains, with Camden Town being skipped by some evening rush hour northbound Edgware branch trains from Charing Cross from 12th March 1934. The following year all southbound trains to Charing Cross stopped again in the morning peak.

An escalation of problems occurred in February 1937, when drivers started a 'go slow' action in protest at speed limit signs. The signs, located on station headwalls, indicated the restriction and the distance before it started; the drivers wanted the signs placed in the tunnels nearer to the point at which they applied. The result of the slower trains was a reduction in line capacity, and so trains were terminated short of their destination to compensate. Matters came to a head on 9th February, when two cars of passengers refused to leave their Morden-bound train at Tooting, and forced the railway to continue their service. The drivers resolved their dispute two days later, but the seeds of insurrection had been sown amongst the passengers.

The drivers held another slow-down in March following changes to the timetables that slightly reduced the running times on the line, but it was not until April that the passengers began their action. It would appear to have started when a signal problem on 5th April created a 10-minute gap in the service south of Edgware in the late evening. In order to fill it so that platforms would not get overcrowded, the traffic controller decided to terminate an Edgware train at Colindale and reverse it. Upon the cries of 'All change' from the platform porters, many passengers complied, but a faction in the front cars refused, shouting 'Stay in your seats and demand to be taken on to Edgware'. Some passengers ran down the train to marshal support from the rear carriages. The porters threatened to fine the passengers for obstruction, but they were undeterred. The driver closed the doors and took the train into the siding. The next train was allowed north to Edgware, and trundled past the troublemakers as they fumed, before their train was shunted back into the southbound platform. The LPTB put out information via the press explaining the need to turn trains short and asking for the forbearance of the passengers. A new timetable was introduced on 17th April with additional trains in both peak hours to help resolve the problems.

A 3-day traffic census was made in 1936, with the express intent of determining the routes passengers used for their journeys. Over 4 million tickets were punched with special stamps at interchange stations, allowing the journeys to be analysed once the tickets were surrendered. This had shown that a very large number of passengers from the Edgware branch changed at Tottenham Court Road, and this led to a rather innovative suggestion: 9-car trains.

A report in September 1936 showed that 9-car trains would accommodate an additional 240 passengers. Plans were enthusiastically drawn up for the lengthening of platforms at Morden, Tooting Broadway, Strand, Leicester Square, Tottenham Court Road, and stations from Brent to Edgware. Unfortunately it was soon found that this was not possible at Strand. It was also decided to restrict the trains to north of Kennington, eliminating Morden and Tooting Broadway from the plans.

It might seem strange that platform lengthening was only considered at some stations, but the logic was sound. The Northern line had 90 platforms in total (74 in tunnel), which would cost over £1¼ million to lengthen sufficiently. The idea of just extending them by 15 feet was briefly toyed with, but the benefit was not worth the cost. The key point of congestion that needed relief was Tottenham Court Road. However, the complexity of operation, as described below, was such that J. P. Thomas sent a memorandum to Lord Ashfield on 7th October 1936 stating that 'the scheme hardly appears to be a practical one ... the probable cost of the palliative of 9-car trains would amount ultimately to so considerable a sum as to form a contribution towards the cost of a new line'. The plan continued though, and Thomas was a key factor in making it work.

A number of tests were run overnight to check the feasibility, and also to see whether 8-car trains might be more practical. It was decided to stick with the nine cars, and for a smaller amount of money the platforms between Golders Green and Burnt Oak were lengthened, as well as the reversing siding at Colindale. The platform extension at Burnt Oak was made of wood, and has since been removed, as have those at Brent and Colindale.

Rather more complicated were the signalling and track changes required. The passing loops at Brent were removed, along with the signal box; the last train to use them operated on 22nd August 1936. The works at Burnt Oak and Edgware took longer to complete, restricting the 9-car trains to operate from Colindale for the first few months.

Of course, the tunnel stations south of Golders Green could only accommodate seven cars, so the service had to be rather ingenious. In the morning rush hour the train stopped in the normal way, with the driver's cab at the end of the platform all the way to Warren Street. This meant that the guard had to be positioned in the seventh car, rather than the rear, necessitating some wiring changes in the train. Passengers in the last two cars remained in the tunnel at these stations. Then at Tottenham Court Road the train stopped with the front two cars in the tunnel, allowing the passengers in the rear cars to leave. These cars remained empty for the rest of the journey to Kennington, with the driver stopping normally again.

The reverse journey in the evening rush hour was slightly different. The front two cars stopped in the tunnel and remained empty between Kennington and Leicester Square, and were only brought into use by the train stopping normally at Tottenham Court Road. This allowed the large number of people wanting the outer stations on the Edgware branch to board. The platform entrance was at the northern end, and this stopping position helped alleviate the congestion that occurred each evening. The front cars then remained in the tunnels again until Golders Green was reached.

Special signs were used on the trains and platforms to notify passengers which cars to use. The sections of tunnel adjacent to platforms where the cars stopped were painted white, and red handrails installed to let passengers know that they were at a station stop (and to prevent them from falling out if the wrong set of doors was opened). A suggestion from the MoT that 'photo-eye' equipment be used to prevent incorrect door operation was politely turned down on grounds of complexity. The train was to carry two lamps and photo-detectors. When the train was in the platform correctly, a fixed mirror would reflect the light into the detector on the end of the train that was in the platform, allowing the doors to open. It was considered to be very difficult to get the alignment correct to make this work reliably, and the engineers were unhappy about the need for bulky and unreliable valve-based amplifiers being fitted to the trains. The mirrors would presumably need regular cleaning to ensure that the system functioned properly. In place of this concept, the possibility of the doors being powered via an extra collector shoe that would only receive current when the cars were in a platform was seriously investigated.

The addition of a frieze that repeated the station name aided identification of stations by passengers. It was pioneered at Tottenham Court Road in 1937. In a throwback to the original station name, Oxford Street appears as a subsidiary name on the bull's eye sign.

The first 9-car train entered passenger service on the morning of 8th November 1937, running from Colindale to Kennington. It was formed of two motor-trailer-motor units sandwiching three trailer cars, and all were repainted to emphasize the new service. Three round trips were operated, departing southbound from Colindale at 07.26 and 08.34, and northbound from Kennington at 18.03. In the morning the return trips northbound from Kennington were operated empty, and in the evening the southbound run was started at Hampstead (from Golders Green depot) and run as a 7-car train all the way to Kennington, with the two rear cars locked out of use.

The new service was deemed a success, and the following February another three were added to the timetable, all operating from Edgware now that the platform lengthening had been completed there. The only platform that could accommodate them was platform 1, and the southernmost 1½ cars would not fit. Passengers arriving in the last two cars had to walk through the train using the communicating doors to disembark. Extensive reports were made about each 9-car train that operated, detailing the passenger loading and any problems that occurred. In the first three weeks only seven passengers were overcarried (i.e., remained in the wrong cars after they should have been emptied of passengers). One of these admitted that he had stayed deliberately to see what would happen.

Overall, the longer trains were certainly seen as being an effective way of relieving congestion without going to the expense of tunnel platform lengthening. Buoyed by the initial success, plans were quickly sketched out for a service of up to 48 trains per hour between Golders Green and Morden via Charing Cross, with many more 9-car trains and a substantial change to the signalling. However, the drawback was that they reduced the number of trains that could be run, as more track space was taken up. Further changes were made in May 1939, when new rolling stock was introduced (covered in a later section). In order to allow drivers to change over, the London Transport Act of 1939 authorized platform extensions at Camden Town, Euston, and Kennington.

Plans were made to extend 9-car working to the Highgate branch and the extensions that were planned for the Northern line. The Bank branch was excluded, as was the line south of Kennington. However, the estimate was that at most eight 9-car trains would be needed. In June 1939 an internal report decided that they should be confined to a few peak-hour workings. Any more than a few trains would mean extensive reconstruction of Camden Town Junction (estimated to cost £106,000), as well as significant changes to signals and stations, and another £200,000 to upgrade the power supply for the line. The additional rolling stock would add another £1.9 million to the cost.

Things changed rapidly with the onset of war in September, and the 9-car workings were soon withdrawn, never to be replaced.

By 1930 consideration was again given to the planned extension to Watford, which had arisen in connection with the enlargement of Edgware station to improve the train services. A third platform and two more sidings would allow all of the trains to run to Edgware. The plans changed with a suggestion that similar improvements to the Edgware service could be delivered by extending the tracks a short distance under Station Road on the line of the Watford extension. However, planning difficulties ensued, and the eventual outcome was the opening of a third platform on the west side of the station on 20th November 1932, together with five sidings to the south.

The local councils north of Highgate looked at the Edgware extension and felt neglected. In July 1933 the Borough Councils of Hornsey and Hendon, Urban District Councils of Barnet, East Barnet Valley, Finchley, Friern Barnet, and the Rural District Council of Barnet sent a petition to the MoT requesting an extension of the branch to Highgate LNER station, where passengers of the main-line railway would be able to transfer to the Underground. This was not a new proposal, having been suggested in Frank Pick's report of 1919 and the preliminary report for the 1924 LER Bill. The MoT discussed the matter with the LPTB, who now dismissed the idea as unimportant in comparison to other schemes under consideration.

The correspondence between the Councils and the MoT rumbled on throughout 1934, with the Councils deploring the lack of action and the Ministry gamely trying to persuade the LPTB to do something. However, the LPTB felt that the extension of the Central London Line into Essex and the electrification of the LNER to Ongar, Ilford, and Romford had to be completed first. In answer to a parliamentary question on 13th June this view was restated by the Minister.

In January 1935 the LPTB wrote to the MoT stating it was desirable to increase travelling facilities towards Muswell Hill and East Finchley, and that they proposed to operate additional buses. However, the MoT blocked this scheme (on the advice of the police) on the grounds of congestion at Highgate station. In consequence, the only action that could be taken was to extend tram route 17 from Archway to East Finchley at busy periods. However, there was a scheme brewing — the New Works Programme.

The mid-1930s saw large-scale planning for improvements to the Underground. The formation of the LPTB, pooling of passenger receipts, and removal of wasteful competition had finally allowed the 'big picture' to be considered. In 1933 the Piccadilly line was extended north to Cockfosters (although the Underground always refers to this as the 'east' end of the line), but this was a single extension planned to relieve congestion at Finsbury Park. The New Works Programme was something on a different scale altogether, encompassing a series of extensions, station rebuilding, and other improvements across the system, at a cost of around £35 million. The Government guaranteed the money, enabling it to be borrowed at a favourable rate by the LPTB. The powers were spread over a number of Acts of Parliament obtained between 1934 and 1939.

An early consideration for the Programme was on the subject of express tubes. As far back as 1905 the Royal Commission on London Traffic had recommended the construction of local and express lines, similar to those of the New York Subway. The local lines would have platforms at every station, but the parallel express lines would only stop at selected locations. The non-stop trains operated on the Hampstead and other tubes provided a similar service, but were constrained by the need to fit in between the timetable paths of 'local' services.

One of the problems for the Northern line was that the Edgware and Charing Cross branches were full to capacity, whereas an additional 12 trains per hour could be fitted onto the Highgate and City branches, had the passenger numbers been sufficient. A report of October 1935 proposed the construction of a new pair of tubes from Waterloo to north of Camden Town on the Highgate branch, with stations at Charing Cross, Leicester Square, and Tottenham Court Road. This would help relieve the overcrowded section south of Camden Town without overloading the Edgware branch by using the spare capacity of the Highgate branch. The ideal situation would be for each pair of tracks in the same direction to be at the same level, although this would mean rearranging the existing lines either side of Waterloo and Tottenham Court Road. South of Waterloo, junctions would allow trains to run to and from Kennington from either line. As a future development it was suggested that a branch could lead from the express line in the Euston area to Finsbury Park, connecting to the LNER (which also had electrification planned). Enfield Chase was a possible northern terminus. In total it was expected to operate 40 trains an hour on the express line.

A schematic map of the express proposals of 1935 as published in the book *London's Secret Tubes*. Express lines are shown between Balham and Kennington, and from Waterloo to Camden Town. Links to Chalk Farm and Finsbury Park were also possibilities. Some stations on the City branch have been omitted for clarity.

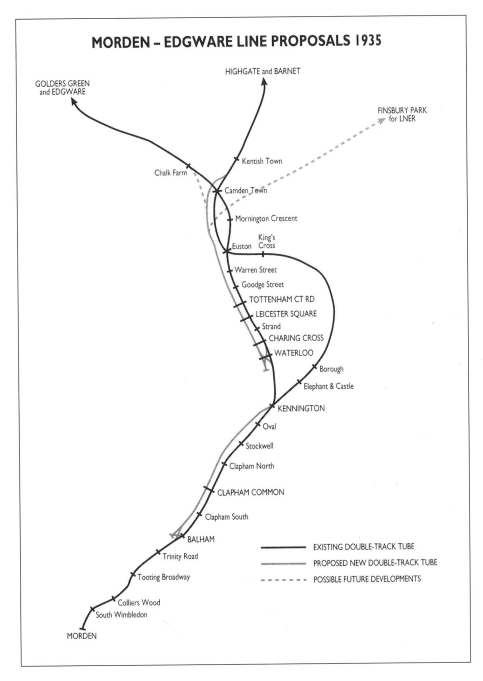

MORDEN – EDGWARE LINE PROPOSALS 1935

GOLDERS GREEN and EDGWARE

HIGHGATE and BARNET

FINSBURY PARK for LNER

Chalk Farm

Kentish Town

Camden Town

Mornington Crescent

King's Cross

Euston

Warren Street

Goodge Street

TOTTENHAM CT RD

LEICESTER SQUARE

Strand

CHARING CROSS

WATERLOO

Borough

Elephant & Castle

KENNINGTON

Oval

Stockwell

Clapham North

CLAPHAM COMMON

Clapham South

BALHAM

Trinity Road

Tooting Broadway

Colliers Wood

South Wimbledon

MORDEN

———— EXISTING DOUBLE-TRACK TUBE

———— PROPOSED NEW DOUBLE-TRACK TUBE

- - - - - POSSIBLE FUTURE DEVELOPMENTS

Following a visit to New York by various LPTB officials in the spring of 1936, the plans were altered. At the northern end the express line was to reach Archway station, but in the south it was to be curtailed at Tottenham Court Road. Junctions at each end would allow trains to be run to and from the rest of the Northern line, but there would be no intermediate stations. The journey time would be 7 minutes, half that achieved by the existing service. The planners were presumably concerned that the large number of additional passengers from the new lines north of Archway might overload the existing trains, in the way that the Edgware extension had caused difficulties to passengers at Golders Green and stations to the south by crowding their trains. The new tube would allow trains travelling the greatest distance (perhaps from as far as Bushey Heath) to be sped quickly into central London, and keep capacity available (if not seats) on the trains calling at Tufnell Park and Kentish Town.

The General Manager, J. P. Thomas, made another suggestion in early 1936 for the relief of traffic north of Golders Green. He proposed a new tunnel from Golders Green to Swiss Cottage, following the route of Platt's Lane and Finchley Road. Two additional platforms would be needed at Golders Green, and at Swiss Cottage a connection would be made to the Bakerloo tunnels that were about to be constructed (linking Baker Street and Finchley Road). Then, with a 'Camden Town' style junction at Baker Street a new branch would diverge south to Victoria. Passengers from Edgware would then be able to travel directly to Victoria, Elephant & Castle (via the Bakerloo line), or via Charing Cross or Bank to Morden. It was an echo of the 1923 scheme to link the two lines, and for similar reasons perhaps best that it didn't happen.

The majority of the New Works that were authorized in the various Acts were planned as extensions to existing lines, in many cases connecting them with existing main-line railways. The extensions relevant to the Morden-Edgware line were:

- Extending the line from Highgate to join the LNER at East Finchley;

- Extending the line north from Edgware to Bushey Heath;

- Connecting the LNER Edgware branch to the LPTB Edgware station;

- Operating trains to High Barnet and Edgware (via Mill Hill), involving electrification of the track and the doubling of the Edgware branch.

- Extending the Northern City line (formerly the Great Northern & City Railway) to the surface at Finsbury Park, and operating trains to Alexandra Palace, East Finchley, and stations beyond.

The thinking behind the extension plans was clear. The LNER tracks north of East Finchley would provide additional traffic for the Highgate branch in an area that was already built up, and for little more than the cost of 1.9 miles of tube tunnel. The Highgate branch was far less congested than that to Edgware. The Edgware branch was already very congested in the peak hours, and so the electrification, doubling, and connection of the LNER Edgware branch would help provide some relief. The extension north of Edgware was more controversial, as it would add to the congestion. However, it was necessary to reach into the countryside in order to get to a site large enough to accommodate a new depot, which was required to house all of the trains needed for the extended line. The lack of housing from Bushey Heath north was in some ways a blessing, as it would prevent the extension causing further overcrowding south of Edgware.

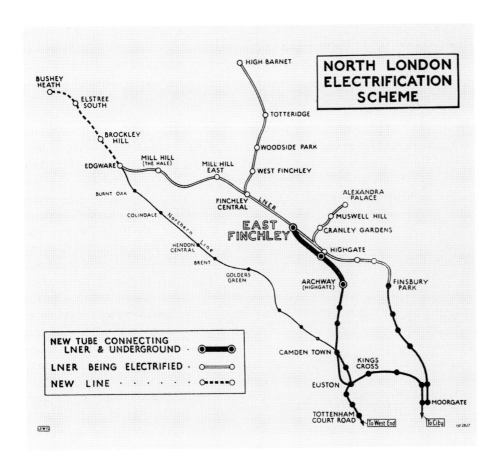

The depot situation had consumed a lot of management time. Sites closer to London had been considered, between East Finchley and Finchley Central, or in Mill Hill, but these had been rejected. The other problem with this extension, out of the control of the LPTB, was the growing pressure for the creation of a 'green belt' around London. The metropolis had sprawled further and further, subsuming villages and towns as suburbs, driven on in part by the spread of the railways. It was in some ways self-defeating: people moved outwards to live nearer the countryside, only to find that within a few years they were in another mock-Tudor suburb. By the 1930s, pressure was being put on the authorities for the ceaseless march of bricks and mortar to be halted so that there would be some open country left around the capital.

Opposition was raised when the Bill came before Parliament, on the grounds of increasing congestion to the south and development to the north of Edgware, but this was ultimately unsuccessful. The first work started in November 1936 when the tunnelling north of Highgate station began.

To the north of Highgate station lay a pair of stabling sidings. The western of these was extended to form the new northbound track; the eastern was adapted as a central reversing siding. The new tunnels ran uphill on a gradient of 1 in 50 to a new station 69 feet beneath Highgate LNER station, which had its platforms made long enough to accommodate 9-car trains. To maintain consistency, the original Northern line terminus was renamed Archway (Highgate) from 11th June 1939.

Rails being laid in the tunnel between Highgate and East Finchley. The man with the loudhailer appears to be co-ordinating the gang of workmen. The rail has an unusual end, forming one half of a 'Brogden' joint (now obsolete). Brackets on the left side of the tunnel will eventually carry cables for power and signalling.

The story of how Highgate station was designed is an interesting one. The original proposal was to link the tube and LNER platforms with a pair of escalators, with another pair then ascending to Archway Road. However, the narrow island platform for the LNER made this impossible to arrange, and, thus, steps were added from the LNER platforms to a hexagonal ticket hall below, where both pairs of escalators would meet — very similar to the final station design. However, the subsurface ticket hall was disliked by the engineers, and so in January 1936 a new plan was prepared. The ticket hall would be on a bridge over the LNER platforms, with a pair of escalators to an entrance in Muswell Hill Road. Another pair of escalators would descend to a subway beneath the platforms, with two more escalators connecting to the tube platforms, and stairs rising to the LNER. The cost of the scheme was less than the original, but the use of six escalators was seen as perhaps extravagant. A rather clever suggestion was that the lower four could be installed as two long machines with intermediate landings which could be floored over giving the appearance of two pairs of escalators. Only two sets of motors and drive gears would be required.

By July this scheme had been dropped, and the original was back in favour, with a pair of escalators flanking a staircase and connecting the tube platforms to a ticket hall beneath the LNER platforms. In January 1937 the LPTB asked permission to omit the staircase, noting that stations such as Clapham North had two escalators in a single shaft. This would save it £7,000. The MoT responded by pointing out that Clapham North had (and still has) a separate spiral staircase, and for such a small saving they did not want the stairs removed from the Highgate plans.

In the same month the architect Charles Holden stepped in and declared the shaft for the upper escalators 'unsightly'. Lifts would be a better solution for the station, he stated. And so plans were created for lifts to descend to the tube platforms from a ticket hall beside the Woodman public house. They were to be sited to the west of the platforms with an intermediate landing, connecting with a subway and stairs up to the LNER platforms.

The constrained site for the lifts meant that smaller lift cars than were usual for the Underground would have to be used, reducing the station capacity. This third plan was therefore dropped in February 1938, and the original scheme again adopted. But now it was pointed out that a subsurface ticket hall would cost about three times as much as one on a bridge.

In an almost unbelievable show of indecision in March 1938 the LPTB presented a completely new set of plans to the MoT. These placed the ticket hall above the LNER tracks on a bridge, with stairs descending to the platforms. The entrance would be level from Archway Road, with four high-speed automatic lifts in a pair of 17ft 6ins diameter shafts descending first to the ticket hall, and then on to the tube platforms below. They would now be situated between the tracks at both levels. A single escalator would descend northwards from the LNER platforms to the new tube platforms; it would carry passengers down in the mornings and back up again in the evenings. Provision for a second escalator was made at the very northern end of the platforms.

The revised plan was explained by the LPTB in terms of time saved. The two flights of escalators in the original scheme would take the average passenger 1 minute 55 seconds to reach the Northern line; with the lifts this would be reduced to 20–70 seconds. The MoT was not convinced, noting that lifts were 'a retrograde step'. They asked for a separate staircase from the deep-level (which the LPTB added in a separate shaft as spiral stairs), and also that the lifts not all be automatic: they worried about passengers not being able to exit at the mid-level ticket hall in time. It was agreed that one pair of lifts would therefore remain under manual control, with the other pair probably running automatically between the upper and lower levels.

The other reason for the new plan was cost saving. It was much cheaper to construct the ticket hall above, rather than below, the LNER tracks. The original estimate was a saving of £40,000–50,000, although as the month of March passed this dropped to £24,830. It looked as if this unusual design would finally be chosen, but then Lord Ashfield stepped in. He was not in favour of lifts, and so this sixth plan was dropped in favour of the original double bank of escalators and subsurface ticket hall. Plans for this design were prepared by Charles Holden, and included a sculpture of Dick Whittington on the roof of the Archway Road entrance. Holden was also asked to provide matching bronze reliefs of Whittington for installation on the platform walls above each roundel.

The final escalator shaft up to Archway Road was a much-simplified version of the design created by Holden, who had planned for the station to have a main entrance near to the Woodman. The two entrances to the station were rather discreet doorways from Priory Gardens and the station car park.

The running tunnels continued northwards following the route of the Archway Road to a point south of East Finchley station. Space did not permit the portal of the southbound tunnel to be widened, which was the normal procedure for preventing an unpleasant pressurization of the air in the train (causing ears to 'pop'). Instead, openings were made in the roof of the tunnel, allowing a gradual increase in pressure.

Looking towards East Finchley from inside the new southbound tunnel, showing the pressure relief openings in the tunnel roof.

The tunnels broke the surface either side of the LNER tracks and crossed the Great North Road before entering the station. This station was completely rebuilt with two island platforms sufficiently long to accommodate 9-car trains. The outer faces of these served trains to and from Camden Town; the inner faces were for trains to and from Finsbury Park. The platforms were accessed from a subway crossing underneath the station and linking to the ticket office. More station offices were constructed in a building that spanned the platforms. The rebuilt station was completed with a statue of an archer firing an imaginary arrow towards central London, sculpted by Eric Aumonier. Very early plans suggested that the tunnels would surface between East Finchley and Finchley Central, presumably to reduce the gradients. A report made in October 1936 determined that East Finchley was the best point to connect as the interchange between existing steam services and the new tube trains would be good. On the opening day only the outer platform faces were ready for trains, there being a few remaining works to complete at the station.

Few changes were made to the other LNER stations northwards to High Barnet. Plans for a new station between East Finchley and Finchley Central, tentatively called Finchley Manor, remained unrealized. Finchley Central — called Finchley (Church End) until 1st April 1940 — was to have been rebuilt with four platforms in a similar style to East Finchley, but the Second World War prevented this from commencing. The down island platform could accommodate 9-car trains, but the works to convert the up platform into an island never progressed beyond a few feet of platform edge constructed at the south end of the eastern platform. Remaining plans show the proposed building with a tall tower structure, probably built with a glass brick front, and a subway under Ballards Lane to a secondary entrance.

Beyond Finchley Central the line divided, with one branch curving to the right, and leading to a terminus at High Barnet. Plans for a reconstruction of this latter station were also cancelled by the war, although its platforms were able to take 9-car trains. A new station between High Barnet and Totteridge & Whetstone was considered for the Willenhall Park area, and was provisionally called Barnet Vale; nothing came of this. No works were carried out at the intermediate stations on the High Barnet branch, although the signals were installed in positions to easily allow platforms to be lengthened to take 9-car trains when these were eventually introduced on this branch.

The branch from Finchley Central to Edgware required more work. It was single track, and so would require doubling as well as the provision of new platforms at Mill Hill East and Mill Hill (The Hale), and some bridge reconstruction. Again, a new station between the two Mill Hills at the Watford Way was considered (referred to as 'Copthall'), but nothing materialized. At the west end a link to the Northern line was needed, allowing trains to reach Edgware station. In order that work could proceed as fast as possible the line was closed on 11th September 1939, with a replacement bus service ferrying passengers between the stations.

Edgware station was to be substantially enlarged at platform level. The original plans called for three new platforms (making a total of six). Trains from Golders Green would have three terminal platforms, with the trains from Finchley using two tracks that would continue northwards to Bushey Heath (one of these tracks would have a platform face at either side). This changed in late 1937 with a new plan that would allow trains from both southern routes access to Bushey Heath. This would allow more operational flexibility, especially for trains from Golders Green needing to

104

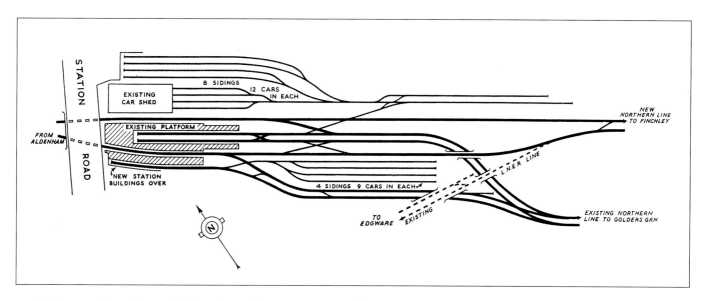

Track diagram prepared for the planned changes in the layout of Edgware station for the unfulfilled extension to Bushey Heath.

reach the new depot. Cross-platform interchange was arranged particularly conveniently so that anyone arriving on a train terminating at Edgware should not have to use stairs to reach a train continuing on to their destination. Further minor changes were made in 1938 in order to accommodate 9-car trains in the platforms.

North of Edgware a route had been reserved for many years, with land having been purchased from the time of the original extension from Golders Green. A long undeveloped strip lay between the houses to take the railway as far as the Edgware Way bypass; beyond lay open countryside. The line was to rise onto a viaduct and cross the bypass, with a station on the far side to be called Brockley Hill, near the junction with the Spur Road to Stanmore. Continuing north-west it would pass beneath Elstree Hill through a pair of tube tunnels 525 yards long before emerging at the south end of Elstree, where Elstree South station would be located. The large depot would be between here and the terminal station at Bushey Heath. This was originally to have been called Aldenham, but following pressure from the local council the name was changed in 1938. However, the depot was always referred to as Aldenham, even though it was some 3 miles from the village of that name, and closer to Elstree.

The only other part of the New Works Programme to affect the Northern line was the connection between the Northern City line at Drayton Park and the surface station at Finsbury Park, and the electrification and resignalling of the surface railway between Finsbury Park, East Finchley, and the branch to Alexandra Palace. All of the trackwork was in place except for the connections to the surface station at Finsbury Park, which were partially completed.

In order to reduce congestion on the Golders Green branch it was decided that trains would run from Bushey Heath via Finchley. Many passengers using Edgware station would find Brockley Hill station more convenient, and would therefore be taking a new route into London. Seven trains an hour would operate in the peaks, with six off-peak. A similar service would operate from High Barnet, giving a train almost every 4 minutes. All of these would run via Charing Cross. In the peak hours an additional seven trains an hour would operate to and from Finchley Central via Bank.

At the outbreak of war on 3rd September 1939 the works were in varying degrees of completion. The tunnels north of Archway (to use the new name) were finished, and tube trains had started to run to East Finchley on 3rd July 1939 (although they did not call at Highgate station, which was not yet complete). The southbound connection ramp to the Northern City line at Finsbury Park had been largely completed, and was used to transfer rolling stock between that line and the rest of the Underground until the 1970s. Structural steelwork for the high-level platforms had also been completed, only to lie as a rusting eyesore until torn down in 1972. Conductor rails had been laid some of the way to Alexandra Palace and East Finchley, as well as the concrete cable posts alongside the tracks. Substation buildings were under construction at Crouch End, Highgate, and Muswell Hill; of these, certainly the first was fitted with the necessary electrical equipment. At Park Junction, where the Alexandra Palace branch diverged, a new signal cabin had opened on 30th July 1939.

The new station building at East Finchley was nearing completion, and the track and signalling alterations to High Barnet were well under way. Some work on laying an additional track had started on the branch to Edgware via Mill Hill, with some Sunday closures from October 1938 to hasten the work. The steam-operated services finished on 11th September 1939 to allow work to progress even faster, and a replacement bus garage was introduced. Substations had been constructed at East Finchley, Finchley Central, Woodside Park, and High Barnet, although they had not been fully equipped; like all of the new substations they were to draw their power from the north London power supply (probably the North Metropolitan Electric Power Supply Company, known as Northmet).

Between Finchley and Edgware another two substations had been completed. One was half way between the two Mill Hill stations, at Page Street, and the other was at Edgware station. At Edgware, work was well underway on the new island platform on the west side, and a new retaining wall was largely complete. A replacement bus station had also been erected in place of the original, which had been on the site of the new platforms. A diversion of the tracks from Golders Green was also being built, which would allow the northbound LNER branch to cross the line to Golders Green. This would in turn facilitate the junction between the two branches south of Edgware station.

North of Edgware the most significant construction work was that for the Aldenham depot, which was well advanced. Vegetation had been cleared from the length of the route, and some brickwork had been laid for the viaduct at Brockley Hill. The substation at Elstree South was also partially complete. Around 230 ft of tunnel had been constructed from the south end of Elstree Hill.

Although it was only six years since Tottenham Court Road had been rebuilt with five new escalators, congestion was still occurring on the Northern line platforms. Plans were swiftly put in place for an additional machine. A passageway was tunnelled parallel to and between the platform tunnels at their northern end, linking to a single Otis M-type escalator ascending to the same intermediate level as the existing pair of escalators. These opened on 27th April 1933.

In the 30 or so years since many of the lines had opened the temperature in trains and stations had risen gently, and the original idea that the trains passing through the tunnels would keep the air circulating had been shown to be inaccurate. In July 1937 the LPTB ordered new fan equipment for installation at Charing Cross,

Hampstead, Belsize Park, and Goodge Street stations. This was not sufficient though, and the LPTB Bill of 1938 included ventilation works at certain stations. On the Northern line, works were proposed at Mornington Crescent, Newington Causeway (near Elephant & Castle), and Balham.

Other work done in 1938 included what *The Times* described as a 'weather maker' plant on the southbound Northern line platform at Tottenham Court Road. Air was blown across pipes containing water kept just above freezing point to cool the platform area. The equipment was installed in a disused lift shaft, and gave the effect of 'placing 50 tons of ice a day on the platform'.

Goodge Street is a deep station with platforms 95ft below the surface, and as one of the quieter stations on the line it was decided to install some experimental automatic high-speed lifts, made by Otis. Two of the original Otis lifts had been removed before the First World War, and the shaft that they occupied was reused for ventilation. Now this shaft was fitted with three smaller lifts, which had an unusual staggered rectangular floorplan to maximize the use of the space in the shaft. Whilst a maximum capacity of 22 people was quoted by Otis, it was difficult in practice to get more than 16 in each. The doors slid round the corner in the lifts, again to get the most out of the space. Unlike the Otis lifts the doors were solid 'to prevent passengers seeing the speed of movement', according to an MoT report.

They were originally planned to operate at 450 feet per minute, but the equipment was specified to have a maximum of 600 feet per minute, reducing the journey time. Experiments showed the operation to be so smooth at the higher speed that the LPTB used this at the MoT inspection and it was duly approved. However, the inspector recommended that LPTB staff, dressed in plain clothes, used the lifts regularly for a time to observe the reaction of the public.

The three lifts came into service on 4th March 1937 and operated from 05.30 until 10.00; two were then run until 17.00, before the third was brought back into service for as long as necessary. Occasionally one of the older lifts was used in the evening peak if required. This was the case when the new lifts failed, a not uncommon event for the first few months. Thirty-eight failures were recorded in the first two months and another 33 in the next 3-month period. A number of small technical changes were made, and many of the faults were the typical 'teething problems' encountered when using new equipment. The MoT remained concerned though, and insisted on a failure report being delivered every three months, and extended their approval for the lifts on a similar basis until July 1938, when the approval was made permanent. The reports had to continue until May 1940 though, by which time the failure level was down to 40 per cent of the average for all lifts on the Underground.

Another of the improvements concerned the noise of the trains in tunnels, which was high. Some measures had been taken, such as the installation of asbestos panels in the sides of the cars, with the idea that this would absorb some of the sound. In early 1935 a trailer car on the line was modified by having its windows sealed and air conditioning fitted; this would eliminate one of the main entry points of noise. It was not a great success and was taken out of service in April 1935. Attention turned to corrugations in the rail surfaces, and other potential sources of noise. Authority was given in September 1937 for 19 miles of track between Kennington, Golders Green, and Highgate to have the rails continuously welded together, eliminating the rail joints that were the source of more noise.

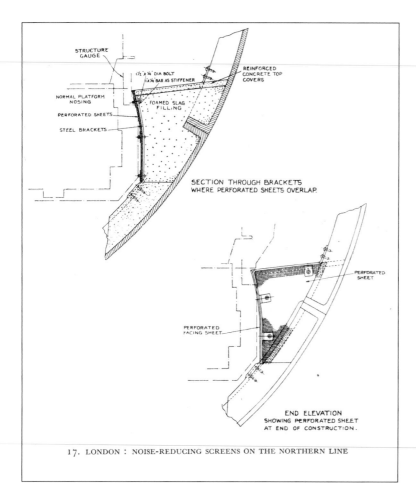

STRUCTURE GAUGE

REINFORCED CONCRETE TOP COVERS

1½" x ¾" DIA BOLT
1" x ¾" BAR AS STIFFENER

NORMAL PLATFORM NOSING

FOAMED SLAG FILLING

PERFORATED SHEETS

STEEL BRACKETS

SECTION THROUGH BRACKETS WHERE PERFORATED SHEETS OVERLAP.

PERFORATED SHEET

PERFORATED FACING SHEET

END ELEVATION SHOWING PERFORATED SHEET AT END OF CONSTRUCTION.

17. LONDON : NOISE-REDUCING SCREENS ON THE NORTHERN LINE

Details of the screens installed between Golders Green and Camden Town to help reduce the noise in the tunnels.

The next part of the noise-reduction plan was put into action on 7th January 1938 when the LPTB signed a contract with Willment Brothers, who were to install noise-reducing screens along 5½ miles of tunnel. The screens were made of asbestos sheeting with foam slag packed behind. Metal brackets were used to fix this to the tunnel walls. The contract was for £15,000 and was to cover the tunnels from Camden Town to Golders Green. It was claimed that the work, combined with the nightly use of a rail-grinding car to smooth the rail surface would prove to be noticeably effective. Whether or not it was successful the programme was interrupted by the war, and was not reinstated (although similar measures were taken when the Victoria line was constructed in the 1960s).

Since 1909 the traffic controllers for the Hampstead, Bakerloo, and Piccadilly tubes had occupied space above Leicester Square station, nominally at 20 Cranbourn Street. This had been enlarged and re-equipped for all of the lines by 1923, and then again in 1929 to cope with the expanding network (although the Piccadilly line controllers were moved to Earl's Court in 1930). In 1939 more changes were made — this time to accommodate the Metropolitan line and also advances in communications. By the end of January 1940 all of the Underground lines were controlled from modernized offices above Leicester Square.

The congestion south of Edgware continued to be a problem as the suburbs grew, and to help alleviate it, the LPTB introduced new trains in the late 1930s. Their rolling stock engineers had designed a new train that had all the control equipment placed below the floor. This, together with the development of a smaller motor, removed the need for the equipment compartment. The new motor cars seated 42, and the trailers 40, giving a 15 per cent increase in capacity for a 7-car train. With the need to increase the capacity of the existing line, as well as providing new trains for the new extensions, it was decided to send the new trains to the Northern line and the Bakerloo line (which was being extended to Stanmore). Deliveries started in May 1938, with Golders Green receiving the first trains. They entered service on the Northern line on 30th June, and had an immediate effect on the crowding levels. The old stock from the 1920s that was replaced was sent to the Central and Northern City lines, although with the extensions of the Central line also delayed by war much of the stock was stabled in depots and sidings around the system for many years.

The new trains, designated 1938 Tube Stock, were formed into seven cars, comprising a 3-car and a 4-car unit. Both units had a motor car with driving cab at the outer ends; a trailer car was placed between them, and the fourth car of the 4-car unit was a new type called a non-driving motor, i.e., having traction motors but no driving cab. At off-peak times a train could be uncoupled and operated as two single units.

The success of the 9-car train experiment led to ninety special cars of 1938 stock being ordered to form ten special trains. This number assumed that they would operate from High Barnet to Kennington, as well as on the Edgware branch. Four trains were required for each, plus two spares. They could not be split into separate units, and as such could only run during the peak hours. This caused some disquiet amongst the rolling stock engineers, who felt that ordering special trains that could only operate a few services each day was an expensive luxury. The equipment on these trains was reduced though, by removing unnecessary duplicate equipment that, on the other trains, provided flexibility in train formation. As fixed blocks they had no need for duplicate driving cabs and complex couplers, and the motors could be grouped more effectively. By June 1939 two of the four 9-car workings were made up of the new rolling stock.

The trains were painted in the standard Underground livery: red bodywork with cream around the windows and a grey roof. Inside, the seats had a striking red and green patterned moquette, the window surrounds were polished wood, and below the window line they were painted green. There were a number of art deco features, ranging from the fluted glass lamp shades to the ventilation grilles inside the car ends and on the outside above the driver's cab. A novel feature for passengers was the introduction of push-button door control. It was intended only for use at surface stations, to avoid letting in cold air if no one wanted to use the doors. Much passenger confusion was caused, as passengers were not used to it and ended up being carried past their stops, and guards did not always activate it on reaching the surface (or left it enabled in the tunnels). It was taken out of use early in the Second World War.

A three-car unit of 1938 tube stock looking very shiny and new, ready to go into service as part of a train on the Northern line.

1939–1945

On Friday 3rd February 1939 terrorist explosions hit the Underground, with two bombs having been deposited in left luggage offices. Seven men were injured in the blasts, which took place early in the morning. The first was at about 05.55 at Tottenham Court Road: a red glow was seen behind the door of the office immediately before the bomb detonated. The office was wrecked, and the door was blown onto the foreman ticket collector, breaking his leg. Another member of staff was taken to hospital with shock.

About 20 minutes later the second device triggered at Leicester Square station. Four staff were injured, as well as a milkman making a delivery. Débris from a dividing wall collapsed onto him, causing multiple abrasions. The left-luggage office and clerks' mess room were destroyed. The damage around the circular ticket hall was extensive, with plasterwork torn from the wall and glass shattered. The top of one escalator was strewn with packets of cigarettes from one of the damaged shops. Total damage to the station was estimated at £650.

Three police constables patrolling nearby rushed to the scene and summoned the fire brigade. A gas pipe had ruptured but was not burning badly, and by 07.10 the fire was out and they were able to depart.

No time was lost in sending police to check all other left-luggage offices at Underground stations. Staff were instructed to open all new items being deposited; any passenger refusing to comply was turned away. Investigations started immediately, and discovered the remains of an alarm clock at Tottenham Court Road, and a battered blue-black fibre case at Leicester Square. All of the staff who had been on duty over the past days were interviewed by the police, who determined that the Leicester Square bomb had been deposited at around 09.00 the previous day.

The bombs were part of a campaign by the Irish Republican Army (IRA) against the British Government. The previous month the IRA had sent an ultimatum demanding the withdrawal of British forces from Ireland; if this was not complied with, then war would be declared. On 16th January seven bombs had been detonated in cities around Britain, and the Underground bombs were a continuation of this. An intensive police hunt was already under way for the terrorists, and arrests were soon made. At a series of heavily guarded court hearings in March and April 21 members of the IRA were jailed for their part in the campaign. However, the explosives and firearms charges related to bombs at Acton and Brimsdown power stations, and at Bankside in Southwark. Although evidence was prepared for the Leicester Square and Tottenham Court Road bombings, the Attorney-General ruled that there was already sufficient evidence without requiring this as well.

Above The design at Leicester Square station, caused by an IRA bomb on 3rd February 1939.

Facing page Camden Town station was seriously damaged by a German bomb on 1st October 1940. This part of the station was never replaced.

111

Underground for Mill Hill East

ON and after Sunday, 18th May, Underground trains (Northern Line) will be extended to Mill Hill East Station (L·N·E·R) via Finchley Central. Trains will run at short intervals to and from Morden, via Highgate (change for steam trains to Finsbury Park), Camden Town, Euston (change for the City), Tottenham Court Rd., Leicester Square, Charing Cross and Waterloo. After 7 p.m. on weekdays, and throughout Sundays, passengers change at Finchley Central.

Mill Hill East & Edgware Buses

★ 240 single-deck service (Edgware and Mill Hill Broadway) will be EXTENDED to Mill Hill East Station and the special (L·N·E·R) buses between Edgware, Mill Hill and Finchley Central Stations will be DISCONTINUED.

★ 240 double-deck service (Mill Hill Broadway and Golders Green) will run AS AT PRESENT: Mill Hill East passengers from Edgware and Mill Hill alight and board at Sanders Lane (Railway Hotel).

Tickets, available by Bus 240 from Edgware and Mill Hill and by Underground from Mill Hill East, will be issued at the ticket offices in Edgware (Underground) and Mill Hill (L M S) Stations. Similarly, tickets will be issued in the reverse direction at Underground and certain L·N·E·R stations.

Advert for opening of Mill Hill East
(*The Times* 15 May 1941)

Below The temporary entrance to Highgate station, opened in 1941.

With the start of war with Germany in September 1939 the pace of work on Underground extensions fell away rapidly. Construction equipment was needed for government works, and steel was needed for the armaments programme. Work ceased north of Edgware, and the depot at Aldenham was turned over to the London Aircraft Production Group, and spent the rest of the war producing Halifax bombers. The partially completed tunnels were used as rifle ranges by the Home Guard.

Of the section between Finchley and Edgware, only the 0.9 miles to Mill Hill East opened, in order to serve the Inglis barracks, from 18th May 1941. Since the second platform and subway had not been completed at Mill Hill East, the branch was operated as a single-track section. The replacement bus service between Edgware and Finchley Central was withdrawn, and instead bus route 240 was extended from Mill Hill Broadway to Mill Hill East from 11th June 1941. The booking office at The Hale closed on the same date, and tickets were thereafter sold from the adjacent London, Midland & Scottish Railway (LM&SR) main-line station.

Works on the High Barnet branch had been nearing completion when war broke out, and so effort was focused here. With freight trains still operating by day and a night-time blackout, conditions were not easy, but even so on the night of 3rd March 1940 some 250 tons of track were moved 120 feet. On 1st April 1940 the current was switched on for trial running, with passenger service starting 13 days later. Six trains an hour operated from High Barnet in the peak hours, with the same number again terminating at Finchley Central. A few steam trains continued to haul freight on the line, but passenger services from Finsbury Park were cut back to terminate at the inner platforms at East Finchley. The LNER parcel service north of East Finchley was replaced by road transport. The standard automatic electric colour light signalling of the LPTB was used throughout the extension (and on the line between East Finchley and Finsbury Park), and special 'distant' signals were used to give the freight trains adequate warning of danger signals ahead. At East Finchley an 'electric train detector' was installed on the southbound approach to the station to prevent the main-line trains from being routed towards the tube tunnels. This consisted of a length of dummy conductor rail; only the tube trains would come into contact with it, and this permitted the signals to clear for the route down to Archway. This was later replaced by three mercury-filled tubes held over the track by a gantry; tube trains would pass safely beneath, but main-line trains would break the tubes, releasing the mercury and setting the signal ahead to danger.

Highgate station was initially used as an air raid shelter during the Blitz, in September 1940, and finally opened to passengers on 19th January 1941. The high-level buildings at the station (on the LNER platforms) had been reconstructed in a more modern style similar to LT stations, and fitted with roundel nameplates by this time, in anticipation of tube trains. The upper escalator structure had caused much difficulty in construction. The clay of the cutting slope turned to slurry in bad weather, causing the subsurface part of the shaft to deform and crack. Subsidence at the top level risked tearing open the 20-inch water main under Archway Road, and so the LPTB was forced to pay for it to be diverted via Hillside Gardens. Dalrymple-Hay, the Consulting Engineer, warned that if the work was not done it risked flooding the Underground workings. The shaft was left unused, its escalator diverted to Bank to replace a machine destroyed by a bomb on 11th January 1941. The entrance on Archway Road was a temporary affair with a wooden staircase leading down to the station entrance serving the car park.

Throughout the 1930s the threat of war posed by Germany had been increasing. The Munich crisis of 1938 brought matters to a head on the Underground, as it was realized that the under-river tunnels were highly vulnerable to aerial bombing, and such action had the potential to flood much of the system. At 20.00 on 27th September 1938 both the Northern and Bakerloo lines were suspended between Strand and Kennington (Northern) and Piccadilly Circus and Elephant & Castle (Bakerloo). On the Northern line, Charing Cross, Waterloo, and half of Kennington stations were closed. Replacement bus services were introduced (mainly for the Bakerloo line), but the short notice given meant that large queues built up at stations south of the river; 100 extra staff were provided to help guide passengers along unfamiliar routes to their destinations. All that LT would say was that urgent structural works were taking place.

In fact, concrete plugs had been made in the tunnels either side of the river. When the Prime Minister Neville Chamberlain returned from Germany with his 'piece of paper' the plugs were removed (the work taking four days), with the stations reopening on 8th October.

The crisis had seriously worried the Underground management, who immediately reviewed every station to ascertain the danger from flooding. It was decided that floodgates were essential, and work started on the Bakerloo tunnels, which were by far the most vulnerable due to their proximity to the river bed. By the outbreak of war the Bakerloo gates were in position but on the Northern line only those at Waterloo were complete (and were demonstrated to the press on 5th October 1939). On 1st September 1939 concrete plugs had again been fitted north of the river, and the work to fit the permanent floodgates continued. The service resumed on 18th December. Had the precautions not been taken and the Northern line tunnels been breached, the flooding would have extended between Clapham Common and Euston.

The original plans for Charing Cross (today's Embankment) were for gates to be installed at both ends of both platform tunnels. However, it was not possible to enlarge the tunnels without closing the line and working under compressed air — the ground around them was heavily waterlogged. The plans were therefore changed, and one set of gates was installed at the south end of Strand station instead. Three other gates were installed so that the entrances to the passenger tunnels at the platform could be sealed off. If the under-river tunnels or the Embankment were breached, then flooding would be confined to the section of tunnels between Waterloo and Strand.

The floodgates were large steel structures that slid across the tracks. Each weighed just under 6 tons, was 13 ins thick, and could hold back a water pressure of over 800 tons. They were electrically operated, and controlled from a small room at Leicester Square station, just off the passageway linking the Northern and Piccadilly lines. Interlocking with the signalling was provided so that a train could not be trapped beneath the Thames, nor collide with a closed gate. Two operators manned each gate at all times; their responsibilities included fitting specially shaped rubber-lined blocks around the rails to form a tight seal when the gate closed. If either of the two electrical power sources failed, then the gates could be closed manually.

Water mains and sewers provided another flooding risk in the event of bombing. Heavy steel flood doors were fitted in the interchange passage between the two lines at Leicester Square. The concern was justified on the night of 21st October 1940 when a bomb penetrated to a depth of 47 feet, the deepest of any that hit London, and

The cover for a leaflet published by the LNER, explaining the changes to the parcel services at High Barnet line stations following the introduction of tube trains.

113

Workmen erecting a floodgate at Charing Cross (now Embankment) station on 26th November 1943. This is the north end of the southbound platform. The frame into which the gate fits is around the mouth of the tunnel, and curved girders combined with lifting tackle enable the gate sections to be swung into position. The temporary name sign on the right is an unusual one. The size of the lettering used for the name is similar to that employed at open air stations during the war to hinder location identification by enemy pilots.

exploded at 22.30. It caused flooding in the vicinity of Mornington Crescent and Euston stations, which were hastily evacuated. Two particularly important trunk telephone cables that used the tunnel were severed in the blast, and Post Office engineers worked in the rising flood waters to effect repairs.

The abandoned tunnel of the Charing Cross loop was also sealed off in September 1939. This was just as well, for a year later it received a direct hit. This was the only under-river tunnel on the Underground to be breached. There were concerns about the pressure behind the bulkheads that sealed it off, and the line was immediately closed between Charing Cross and Waterloo. Inspection of the crater in the river bed by divers showed that an 8ft length of tunnel was fractured, and concrete and clay were used to seal the hole.

Tube stations had first been used as air raid shelters when the Zeppelins started to drop bombs on the capital in 1915. It was not surprising when people took to the stations again in 1940 when the Blitz began. However, the Government and the LPTB felt very strongly that this should be discouraged, as it would disrupt the operation of the railways. Staff were instructed to turn away those who were not genuine passengers, a measure overcome by people purchasing the cheapest tickets and then remaining in the station. By mid-September 1940 the officials had become resigned to the fact that people were going to shelter in the stations, and efforts started to improve the facilities and prevent the shelterers from disrupting the railway operation. Beds and sanitation were gradually installed. Later in the year 'Tube Refreshment' trains operated, carrying tons of food and drink to the shelterers. These were introduced on the Central line, and reached the Northern line in mid-November, operating from Golders Green depot to Camden Town, and then up to Highgate. Power sockets and water supplies were installed at platform level, and an army of female LPTB staff in green dresses and red headscarves carried giant teapots (1d per cup) and trays of fruit, cakes, pies, and buns (at 1d–2d each).

Aside from the use of open stations as shelters, a number of disused stations were opened for this purpose. On the parts of the Northern line with which this book is concerned these additional shelters were at South Kentish Town and Highgate. The use of the latter station has already been mentioned. At South Kentish Town beds and a first aid post were installed, with shelterers gaining access via the spiral stairs, as the lifts had been long-removed. A low wall with metal mesh above was constructed along the edge of each platform to prevent access to the tracks. Unusually, the work was carried out by St Pancras Council: normally the LPTB was responsible for preparing its property for the shelterers. Once the work was complete, the shelter opened on 10th February 1941.

Although only 500 wooden and canvas bunks had been installed, it was not uncommon for 720 people to use the shelter. Conditions were grim, and when the shelter was inspected by a doctor on 15th December 1941 he recommended that the station be used in emergencies only because of its state. Dirt and dust were blown in through the wire mesh, and the facility was infested by bugs (type not given) that lived in cracks in the rough walls along the platform edges. His recommendations were to cover in the wire mesh, fill the cracks and holes in the wall and spray the walls with insecticide, and replace the bunks nearest the tracks by steel bunks (which were easier to clean).

Six months later the Council finally approved the works, and the mesh was plastered over. Distemper was used on the walls, and insecticide sprayed. However, the LPTB had no spare steel bunks, so these could not be changed; instead, the existing bunks were removed to the cyanide chamber to kill any insects, before being put back into the shelter. Although improving the ventilation was considered, the Council decided that it could not afford the necessary £700.

The bunks were finally replaced in late 1943, when the closure of other station shelters freed up the steel beds. The shelter then continued in use until May 1945, when it, along with all of the others finally closed. Arrangements were rapidly made for the removal of bunks, first aid posts and other facilities from the open stations. The three disused stations (South Kentish Town, as well as City Road on the C&SLR and British Museum on the Central line) were to be 'dealt with later, provided that they are safeguarded against outside interference and any inflammable material at once removed', according to an LPTB report.

The intensive bombing of London in late 1940 caused the Government to consider the construction of more deep-level shelters. With an eye to the future, it was decided that they should be constructed in locations that would allow their use after the war as part of a series of new tube railways. Lord Ashfield confirmed to the Government that the Central and Northern lines were the highest priority for parallel express tubes (as had been discussed in 1935/36). Camden Town to Tottenham Court Road was one of the three such tubes he proposed (the others were between Kennington and Balham on the southern section of the Northern line, and between Bank and

Holborn on the Central line). Whilst the running tunnels were to be placed beneath the existing tunnels, at stations he anticipated the new platforms flanking the old (which would therefore need reconstruction to place the platforms on the outside, allowing cross-platform interchange with the express trains). The LPTB took responsibility for their construction, but at the expense of the Government. This was initially estimated at £1.5 million, but by the time they were completed this figure had doubled.

It was decided to construct the shelters at stations that would not receive express platforms; this would allow them to be built as pairs of tunnels 1,400ft long and 16ft 6ins in diameter, beneath the platform tunnels of existing stations. With the plans for express tubes from the mid-1930s in mind, the Northern line locations considered were at: Belsize Park, Camden Town, Mornington Crescent (dropped in favour of Camden Town), Warren Street (dropped in favour of Belsize Park because of poor subsoil), Goodge Street, Leicester Square, Oval, Stockwell, Clapham North, Clapham Common, and Clapham South.

The shelter at Leicester Square was a late addition to the list, and then rejected in March 1941, probably because it was an interchange station, making the works more complicated, as the Piccadilly line is below the Northern at this point. Work had already started on the other shelters by this time, with the work at the three Clapham sites and Goodge Street being well advanced. Oval was already encountering problems with water ingress, with both shafts sunk and a very small length of tunnel completed. The difficulties here caused it to be abandoned and sealed up in August 1941, although part of the northern shaft was used in the early 1950s to provide additional ventilation for Oval station. Acting on their own initiative, the Metropolitan Borough of Islington proposed two other shelters at Archway and Tufnell Park stations, but government funding was refused.

The shelters were accessed from shafts situated about one-quarter of the way along from each end of the tunnels, and the tunnels themselves were divided into two levels, with lavatories and medical posts in short side tunnels. The original estimate was that 9,600 people would be accommodated, but this was later reduced to 8,000 to improve the conditions. Staircases linking the shelters with the stations above would be provided, but were not for general use. Large, ugly concrete blockhouses with air filtration systems were installed at the top of the shafts, which were fitted with stairs and small lifts. Again, the lifts were not for general use, as they would not be able to handle the anticipated number of shelterers in an acceptable time.

Work progressed quickly, and the shelter at Camden Town was completed by July 1942, and in use by October. Goodge Street was completed that month, and Belsize Park was ready in January 1943. Initially they were kept in reserve to minimize costs, and it was only Goodge Street that was partially brought into use as the headquarters for General Eisenhower. During 1943 the other shelters were used for billeting servicemen. Only when the V-rocket air raids of 1944 started, did the Government finally allow the public to shelter. Goodge Street retained its military purpose, but Camden Town opened to the public on 16th June 1944, and Belsize Park on 23rd July. They remained in use until 7th May 1945, by which time the number of people using them had dropped considerably. Thereafter the LPTB maintained the shelters on behalf of the government.

There were a number of incidents of bombing affecting the former Hampstead Tube during the war. During the Blitz the first incident was when a bomb damaged

Colindale station's street building was completely destroyed by a bomb probably intended for nearby Hendon airfield. This view shows the rubble being cleared a few days after the incident.

Tottenham Court Road station on the night of 24th September 1940. Two bombs probably targeted at Hendon airfield hit Colindale station in the same month, causing severe damage. Also in September the service was suspended between Hendon and Brent for 14 days because of a bomb on the line. Amazingly, no damage was caused to the railway when it finally exploded, and services were rapidly restored.

On 14th October 1940, a bomb demolished part of Camden Town station, killing five people. One-third of the Camden High Street façade was lost, and although the remaining façade was subsequently rearranged, the missing section of building was never replaced.

One other casualty of the war was the 9-car train experiment. The longer trains were stopped from the beginning of hostilities. The block trains of 1938 stock each had two trailers removed to form 7-car trains that could operate almost normally; however, they could not be uncoupled for off-peak operation because of their formation. Because all seven of the remaining cars were fitted with motors these trains would have been too powerful, and so the motors were removed from two of the non-driving motor cars in each train. The only difference that could be seen by the passengers was that the guard rode in the fifth car, rather than the seventh, due to the special wiring in place for 9-car operation.

The trailer cars that were removed were reused from 1944, although some had to wait until more rolling stock was ordered in 1949. This order was for a mix of cars that, combined with the trailers and also some experimental trains from 1935, would form new trains to run on the Bakerloo and Piccadilly lines. This in turn allowed rolling stock from these lines to be transferred to the Central line to boost the services. Also dropped during the war was the practice of uncoupling trains between the peaks. The activity was labour-intensive, and with the reduction in staffing levels it became impractical to continue.

POST-WAR DECLINE

Britain had changed after the end of the Second World War. The conflict had been terribly expensive, and the Government was quick to reassess its spending plans. The most significant works remaining on the Underground were the half-completed parts of the New Works Programme on the Northern and Central lines. The Central line works were seen as having greater priority, and so these resumed quickly once hostilities ceased. The Northern line had to make do with the issuing of statements declaring the works would resume as soon as possible.

The maps issued by the LPTB in the late 1940s, which included the lines to Alexandra Palace and Bushey Heath, show the works were intended for completion in their entirety. In the planning department, work continued: the site for Bushey Heath station was changed to a new alignment which had originally been proposed in 1943 and which would make it easier to extend the line further towards Watford.

Opposite Hampstead in the late 1940s, showing the tube station in largely original condition.

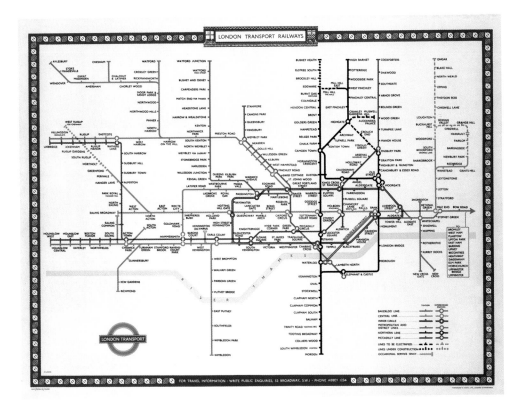

Underground map of 1947 showing the uncompleted Northern line extensions not yet dead. The Central line extensions shown were a greater priority and all were opened.

119

A report written in early 1946 predicted that the railway would open from Mill Hill East to Edgware by June 1948. The line to Bushey Heath was placed fifth in order of priority for the scarce funds of the day. However, planning outside the railway companies was about to have a serious impact. The Greater London Plan was drawn up in 1944 by Patrick Abercrombie, who was Professor of Town Planning at University College London, and had co-authored the County of London Plan in 1943.

The Greater London Plan had proposed the creation of a green belt around London. The unrestricted growth of the 1920s and 1930s had created a worry that London would continue to sprawl outwards, absorbing towns and villages and concreting over the countryside. The green belt was a circular area around the built-up part of London in which new development was to be severely restricted. Edgware and Finchley were on the edge of this belt, making the extension of the line into it far less attractive. With construction costs rising and potential development around the new stations curtailed, the remaining works were not economically attractive.

And so it was on 7th October 1950 that the LPTB announced that the Bushey Heath extension had been abandoned. It noted that electrification from Mill Hill East to either Edgware or Mill Hill (The Hale) might be considered later, as might a short extension to Brockley Hill. The original justification in the 1930s for the extension — namely to reach the 'essential' new depot at Aldenham — had been demonstrated to be unnecessary (as the line had coped throughout the war without this facility), and the new buildings were converted from aircraft factory into bus overhaul works.

The decision had been taken at least a year beforehand though, since in late 1949 the tunnelling shields under Elstree Hill had been removed and the tunnels sealed. In 1954 a further announcement was made abandoning the extension permanently. The land north of Edgware station was sold for building works. The London Transport Act for 1964 authorized a 21-yard extension of the tracks serving platforms 2 and 3 to a point under Station Road. The works, completed in 1966, increased the safety margin required in connection with new signalling.

Bus route 240 (later 240A) serving Mill Hill East, Mill Hill (The Hale), and Edgware continued to run, and Underground tickets were issued (headed LNER) as though the railway were open. Some passengers even held season tickets for the route, although these were only issued to existing ticket holders after around 1954. The LM&SR station at Mill Hill Broadway (in place of the closed facilities at The Hale) sold the railway tickets used on the bus until around 1955. A line had to be printed on the ticket under the station of origin, otherwise the bus conductors would not accept them. This feature was in place because it was cheaper to use a railway ticket on the route than it was to buy a bus ticket.

The railway was finally closed on 1st June 1964 with the withdrawal of the few freight trains that ran. The track was promptly lifted and sold (at a profit) for scrap by British Railways (BR — who were still the owners), and the land auctioned off. A few members of the public protested to their MPs and BR, and some even suggested new uses for the line, but to no avail. The construction of the M1 motorway severed the track bed between Mill Hill East and Edgware just to the east of Mill Hill (The Hale) station. The special tickets continued to be issued until 1969.

Some of the sections of viaduct built either side of the Brockley Hill station site were demolished in 1959; the piers for some arches can still be seen in a field north of the Edgware Way. The bricked-up and partially flooded entrances to the tunnels under Elstree Hill disappeared without trace beneath more works for the M1.

120

One other idea that has appeared occasionally is that of separating the Northern line into two separate and independent lines to reduce the complexity of operating it. Because of the track layout at Kennington it would be most logical for Bank branch trains to operate to Morden, with Charing Cross trains terminating at Kennington and reversing using the loop. The junction at Camden Town is so well designed that either northern branch could connect to either central section without conflict. However, it would make most sense for the Edgware branch to run via Charing Cross, as this line would then be able to use Golders Green depot whilst the Barnet and Bank line would have Morden depot.

The idea has been considered, and taken as far as surveying passengers to get their opinions. The majority are not in favour, as they value the choice that the current line gives them. From an operating viewpoint congestion at Camden Town would increase considerably (probably to an unsafe degree) with passengers transferring between lines, as the platforms are not adjacent. Kennington would also see more people changing, but has a better cross-platform layout. Expensive and difficult construction works would be needed at both stations though, making the proposals even less attractive.

The Northern line station at Strand closed to the public on 16th June 1973. This was one of the first public signs of the works to construct the Jubilee line. Strand was fairly close to Trafalgar Square on the Bakerloo line; the new Jubilee platforms would be between and below the level of those on the existing lines. The work would result in a single station, to be called Charing Cross. Escalators would serve all platforms, and the stations would get a complete refurbishment. The Underground station at the river end of Charing Cross main-line station was subsequently renamed Embankment. The escalators connecting the ticket hall beneath the main-line station forecourt with the Northern and Jubilee platforms had to cut through the lift shafts at Strand and so the station closed for almost six years whilst the work progressed. In that time new platform décor was provided – a set of murals depicting the construction of the mediæval Charing Cross, created by David Gentleman.

Just below the surface, the new ticket hall was constructed using plastic surfaces in a range of bright primary colours (a theme of the Jubilee line decoration, in contrast to the drab greys used on the Victoria line). New subways connecting with the north side of the Strand and the main-line station were built at the same time on behalf of the Greater London Council.

When the Jubilee line was constructed at Charing Cross the rest of the station was refurbished and redecorated. The Northern line platforms were provided with these murals, by David Gentleman. They are in the style of woodcut prints, and depict the construction of the Charing Cross.

A FRAGILE RENAISSANCE

The 1980s were a new high point for the Underground. In 1985 it was transferred to a new company, London Underground Ltd (LUL), which was owned by London Regional Transport, a Government agency.

After decades of decline, passenger numbers were at last rising again, and money was being found to pay for (in some cases long-overdue) refurbishments. The most dramatic changes occurred in 1984 at Tottenham Court Road, where much of the station was retiled in a modern mosaic by Eduardo Paolozzi, capturing the vibrant themes of the streets nearby. Leicester Square was retiled with a cinema theme: film 'sprocket holes' run along the top and bottom of the platform walls. Plans to include Hollywood stars and scenes from famous films were dropped when a sponsor could not be found.

In 1987 the Charing Cross branch platforms at Euston were refaced in vitreous enamel panels incorporating colourful elements from the heraldic arms of the Duke of Grafton, who has the subsidiary title Earl of Euston. Embankment also received enamelled panels, featuring a variant of the 'streamer' design used elsewhere on the station.

Away from the central area, Belsize Park lost its Leslie Green ticket hall in 1990. The need to rebuild the ticket hall to include the latest Underground Ticketing System equipment (ticket gates and machines, as well as a secure ticket office) co-incided with the replacement of the lifts. A programme of work provided a new ticket hall tiled in shades of grey with coloured patches marking lifts and ticket machines. It is an interesting design, but looks slightly dated now.

Another station requiring lift replacement was Mornington Crescent. The lifts were taken out of service in summer 1990, but the station remained open. The £7 million to pay for new lifts was found when the Government increased its grant to LUL in 1991, and so the station closed on 23rd October 1992 to allow work to commence. It was estimated that it would take around 15 months to complete.

Less than one month later the Government announced a 30 per cent cut in funding to LUL. The *Evening Standard* described it as a 'Betrayal of London', and the Underground management immediately started to look at what projects could be cut. Mornington Crescent, being a less busy station, had its works suspended, with the closure extended until June 1995. However, by mid-1994 the only work that had taken place was the removal of the old lifts, and it was being rumoured that the station would never reopen, although the official line was that the wait would be another two years.

Facing page The unusual design of the ticket hall at Belsize Park following the installation of new ticket machines in 1989. The ticket gates were added in 2000.

Work finally restarted in 1996, with the new lift equipment being craned into the station overnight. The plan now included replacement tiles through the station, comprehensive CCTV coverage of all areas, and restoration of heritage features. At platform level the distinctive tiling pattern was not renewed, but the tiling retained other original features. Long-disused passageways at low level reopened, removing conflict between flows of passengers entering and exiting the platforms.

The station was reopened on 27th April 1998 at 09.45 by the stars of BBC Radio 4's comedy panel game *I'm Sorry, I Haven't a Clue*. This long-running radio show features a game called Mornington Crescent, and so their attendance was very appropriate. The public was admitted to the station from 12.00.

One station change that was most unwelcome was the closure of the Finchley Road entrance at Golders Green from Christmas Eve 1997, following a battle that had lasted for some years. LUL noted that the cost of installing ticket gates was too high, but this did not placate the objectors who gathered more than 1,000 signatures on a petition calling for it to be reopened – to no avail.

The 1938 tube stock had left passenger service on the Northern line on 14th April 1978. It seemed that the end was near for these trains, which only remained on the Bakerloo line. However, the rise in traffic in the 1980s led to increased pressure on the train service, and it was soon found that the Underground had insufficient rolling stock. The pressure was increased by the rolling programme for converting trains to one-person operation; this involved trains being out of service whilst the necessary changes were made to them.

The answer was to rehabilitate the last five trains of 1938 stock that remained on the Underground (by now most had been withdrawn and scrapped). Extensive refurbishment was carried out, and the trains were repainted into their original colours, with red and cream bodywork, grey roofs, and the interiors in cerulean blue and off-white. The first train entered service on 15th September 1986, and the last on 19th January 1987. Four were planned for use at any one time, with one as a spare. They were troublesome to operate, and lasted until 19th May 1988. The final run was operated by the train that had entered service first, known by its nickname of the *Starlight Express*. It had been the last train withdrawn from the Bakerloo line, and included one car that had been part of the very first train to enter service on 30th June 1938, almost exactly 50 years before its final service trip. It remains in London, preserved as part of a 4-car train of 1938 tube stock at London Transport Museum's Acton Depot.

A large project to provide the complete renewal of trains and signals on the Central line in one large programme of works had been started in the 1980s, and it was decided to repeat the process with the Northern line. The necessary project team was put together in 1989, and began to plan the new trains and signalling system, with an expected cost of over £700 million. A leaflet was quickly distributed to passengers informing them of the plans, and showing illustrations of the proposed new trains. This good start was marred at the end of 1990 by a recession that forced spending cutbacks across the Underground, and work was delayed for over a year before restarting.

Less than a year later the spending cuts resulting from the funding cut in November 1992 had a serious effect on the project. Wilfred Newton, chairman of London Transport, stated that 'it would not be feasible to start on such a massive project in a climate of inconsistent, unreliable funding'. In January 1993 a hit list of

The cover of a leaflet from 1995 outlining planned improvements to the Northern line.

We're opening up
a New Northern Line

You can't beat the Tube

projects to be cut was announced. As well as the postponement of works at Mornington Crescent, the Northern line also suffered a delay in train refurbishment (until 1995/96), a year's delay for new escalators at Kentish Town and station modernization on the Edgware branch, and the cancellation of signal modernization. The overall project was now expected to start in 1996. Another leaflet was prepared, describing the now £1 billion project. As well as the new trains and signalling, station modernization, upgraded communication links, and rebuilt substations were listed. The project was predicted to be completed by the end of 2001.

In the late 1980s an extensive programme of rolling stock refurbishment began on the Underground. Although driven by the need to ensure that all materials were as fire-resistant as possible (following a tragic fire at King's Cross in 1987), the opportunity was taken to improve the look of the trains for passengers. The interiors were redecorated and to help protect against the growing scourge of graffiti (which could not be entirely erased from the aluminium surface of the trains) the exteriors were painted in a standard livery. However, with most of its trains over 30 years old it was not worth investing too much in the Northern line. Work on its trains started in 1989 and was more extensive on the 1972 trains, as they had a longer life expectancy. The changes to the 1959 trains were principally to improve the safety of the trains by adding passenger alarms and public address systems. This work was carried out at Highgate depot, which was reopened from 23rd January 1989. One train was painted into the new red, white, and blue corporate livery, and in 1990 one was painted into the livery used in 1923 on Standard Stock. This became known as the 'Heritage' train, and was used in the C&SLR centenary celebrations in 1990. The rest of the trains retained their rather neglected look.

The need to provide new trains was very apparent to passengers, even though reliability was high. A tender was issued, and on 8th December 1994 it was announced that GEC-Alsthom (renamed Alstom — with no 'h' — from 22nd June 1998) were the winners. For the first time a Private Finance Initiative (PFI) was to be used; under this arrangement the manufacturers would continue to own and maintain the trains, and would lease them to London Underground. This would save LU having to find around £400 million in the short term, and would also give the manufacturer a strong incentive to make the trains as reliable as possible. The Northern line depots would be transferred to GEC-Alsthom, as well as all of their staff.

The design of the new trains (called 1995 Tube Stock) was based closely on that for the extended Jubilee line, which was being built by the same manufacturer. One of the first cars to be delivered was exhibited on a float at the Lord Mayor's Show on 9th November 1996. For the first time on the Northern line the trains were fitted with externally-hung sliding doors, space inside for wheelchair users, and electronic displays informing passengers of the next station and destination for the train.

The first complete train arrived on the Underground on 20th December 1996, and testing began. On 12th June 1998 the first train entered passenger service. It was not all plain sailing from here though, as the 1959 Tube Stock remained in service until 27th January 2000. The usual teething problems occurred, and in December 1998 the Line Manager issued a letter to all passengers explaining the problems and asking for their patience. The new trains drew more power than their predecessors, because of their higher rates of acceleration. With more trains operating, the power supply for the line also needed upgrading, and so 16 substations were re-equipped between 2000 and 2005. A new substation was also provided at Angel.

Another leaflet was issued to announce the introduction of the new trains and explain their features.

INDEX

Note: There may be more than one reference on the page indicated. *Italicised entries refer to illustrations*.